God is Waiting for our Success

Equipped for Spiritual Warfare

DR. ALAN PATEMAN

By Dr. Alan Pateman

BY DR. JENNIFER PATEMAN

AVAILABLE FROM APMI PUBLICATIONS, AMAZON.COM AND OTHER RETAIL OUTLETS

Equipped for Spiritual Warfare

DR. ALAN PATEMAN

BOOK TITLE:
Equipped for Spiritual Warfare
(Originally published as The Reality of a Warrior)

WRITTEN BY Dr. ALAN PATEMAN
ISBN: 978-1-909132-13-9
eBook ISBN: 978-1-909132-14-6

Published By:
APMI Publications
In Partnership with Truth for the Journey Books **33**
Email: publications@alanpateman.com
www.AlanPatemanMinistries.com

Acknowledgements:
Author/Design/Senior Editor/Publisher: Apostle Dr. Alan Pateman
Editing/Proofreading/Research: Dr. Jennifer Pateman
Computer Administration/Office Manager: Dr. Dorothea Struhlik
Cover Image Credit: Sirle K, www.PosterMyWall.com

Unless otherwise indicated, all scriptural quotations are from the HOLY BIBLE, NEW INTERNATIONAL VERSION ®. NIV ®. Copyright © 1973, 1978, 1984 by the International Bible Society. Used by permission of Zondervan Publishing House. All rights reserved.

*Where scriptures appear with special emphasis (**in bold,** italic or <u>underlined</u>) we have edited them ourselves in order to bring focused attention within the context of this subject being taught.*

❖

Table of Contents

❖

Acknowledgement

To Reverend Dr Tunde Bakare Pastor of The Citadel Global Community Church Lagos Nigeria *(formerly known as The Latter Rain Assembly)*, who impacted my personal life and ministry.

Back in 1992 he opened a significant door to the entire continent of Africa for me. I am forever grateful to this man of God.[1]

❖

Preface

This book, *Equipped for Spiritual Warfare* is the NEW UPDATED VERSION of what was formerly known as *The Reality of a Warrior,*[1] published back in 1991. In retrospect, I can honestly declare that this book made literal strides around the globe, especially *(but not limited to)* the African continent. The impact of which has exceeded my wildest expectations.

It all began over three decades ago, when I was discovering for myself what it meant to live and minister in the authority of Christ's name and in the power of His Spirit. But you have to understand, that although I was loaded with revelation and was seeing God's power flow through my ministry, still the prospect of writing a book was daunting.

During my formative years I struggled with acute dyslexia, the implications of which involved severe anxiety, *(at just the mention of writing down some of my own thoughts on paper!)* My younger years had convinced me, *(with the help of some misguided teachers)* that I'd never amount to anything in these areas, especially not in the realm of academia. BUT this could not have been further from the truth!

To date I've published over 36 books, along with university curriculums and many other teaching materials and articles etc. When it comes to my first book, the whole painstaking process took me no less than four years! Today that seems a crazy amount of time, but once I managed to publish this book; that which had been written in relative obscurity, produced the most powerful breakthrough imaginable. The impact of which, I'm still living in today.

You see God is waiting for our success. He is waiting for us to push through all the struggles and to rise from the obscurity that life has held us captive to.

Not long after the publishing of this book, I visited a church in London *(Victory Church)* pastored by Rev Michael Bassett. It was a popular city church and famous for hosting all the powerful international gifts. It was there I was first introduced to Rev Tunde Bakare *(of Latter Rain Assembly, Nigeria),* while he was preaching in London.

Some time later and unbeknownst to me, Tunde had been handed a copy of my book, while back home in Nigeria. He said, "I took one look at that book, turned it over, saw your face and heard God say, 'You have to invite this man to Nigeria!'" Before I knew it, I was being met at Lagos' airport by security guards who placed me into a waiting Mercedes and took me to Latter Rain Assembly, where my host was waiting for me. The rest is history.

This was the open door God used to send me into the continent of Africa. It's true to say, that our destinies are subject to divine connections and the open doors that God Himself engineers. AND I want to thank all those obedient and discerning doorkeepers, who understand that God's Kingdom must move forwards this way.

Today I run an International University Program (*LifeStyle International Christian University*) that caters for correspondence students and those being taught on-campuses in different countries around the world. I am happy to report that most students that we have today, are active pastors, which means we get to impact many more people.

The long-term influence of our teaching materials is multiplied countless times over, as many local pastors use them to inform and teach their own congregations, collectively totalling thousands.

God is the Best Strategist,

Now it's Your Time!

❖

Introduction

Many Christians think that they are out to make **converts,** but that is not our commission. In fact the bible tells us to go and make **disciples** of all nations, baptizing them in the name of the Father and of the Son and of the Holy Spirit, and **teaching them to obey everything I have commanded you** *(Matthew 28:19-20)*.

It seems to me the devil doesn't want us Christians to understand who we are in Christ. Our job is to abide in Christ, and if we do, the Holy Spirit will produce fruit, and this fruit is the result of our obedience.

As we become more obedient to the Lord and learn to walk in His ways, our lives will change. The biggest change will take place in our hearts; the overflow of this will be a new outworking *(thoughts, words and actions)*, representative of that change. The change we seek is done from the inside out, through the power of the Holy Spirit. It isn't something we can conjure up on our own. Remember that revelation *(Rhema)* is the transformative Word and when you eat of Him, you gain His life, *(power and resurrection)*.

"When the apostolic ministry is restored to the church builders, God's people will become preeminent *(highly distinguished and outstanding)*. Consequently, local churches will become far more stable and powerful. **When everyone knows their place and are cemented there,** it will take a lot to pry them out again.

You can steal stones from a pile, but try stealing one that has been concreted into a building."[1]

That's why Satan will do everything he can to keep Christians from learning the truth found in the Word; he will fight us more on this, than anything else. He knows that once we learn the truth, his heyday is over.

This book *Equipped for Spiritual Warfare* helps all believers and disciples of Christ to become warriors for these end times and to know where they belong... *"This is a new commission and direction I am giving unto you."* Teaching you how to stand in His authority and dunamis power as an heir in Christ Jesus.

Dr. Alan Pateman

CHAPTER 1

The Name of Jesus

Every Tongue shall Confess

He has now been given the greatest of all names! The authority of the name of Jesus causes every knee to bow in reverence! Everything and everyone will one day submit to this name — in the heavenly realm, in the earthly realm, and in the demonic realm.

Every tongue will proclaim in every language: "Jesus Christ is Lord Yahweh," bringing glory and honor to God, his Father! *(Philippians 2:9-11 TPT)*

God has highly exalted Jesus above every name and as the scripture above says, every knee shall bow and every tongue shall confess of those in heaven and on earth that

Jesus Christ is Lord and that includes Satan and his demonic hosts.

Our spiritual authority is based upon the blood of the Lamb and the understanding that Satan's claims and rights were destroyed by Christ's death and blood shedding at Calvary.

Satan is already defeated and we have the authority to speak directly to him and his demons in Jesus' name. Matthew 16:23 told us how Jesus spoke directly to Satan by saying, *"Get behind me, Satan" (when Peter allowed himself to be an instrument of the devil).* Also at the time of His temptation in the wilderness, Jesus spoke with authority directly to Satan *(Matthew 4:1-11).*

In verse 10 Jesus said to him *"away from me Satan, for it is written: worship the Lord your God, and serve Him only."* Then the devil left Him *(verse 11).*

James also tells us; *"...resist the devil and he will flee from you" (James 4:7).* Satan will flee when we speak not in our own authority but in the authority, which Jesus has given us in the power of His name. Jesus has given us authority over all power of the enemy.

In seeing Satan He said,

> *I saw Satan fall like lightening from heaven. I have given you authority to trample on snakes and scorpions and to overcome **all the power of the enemy;** nothing will harm you...*
>
> *(Luke 10:18-19)*

Jesus however, goes on to say in verse 20, not to rejoice that the spirits submit to you, but to praise God and rejoice that your name is written in heaven.

Satan will try and do all he can to frighten and prevent believers from using the weapons that God has given. He does not care what you say about him, he does not fear or flee from you unless you speak in the authority of the name of Jesus, and with full reliance upon the victory won at Calvary.

The Blood

Jesus came as the sacrificial Lamb, *"For Christ, our Passover Lamb, has been sacrificed..." (1 Corinthians 5:7)* To understand fully the implications of what happened at Calvary when Jesus died on the cross *(the second Passover)* we need to look in Exodus 12:1-6, 11-13, to the First Passover.

The Lord said to Moses and Aaron in Egypt,

> *This month is to be for you the first month, the first month of your year. Tell the* **whole community** *of Israel that on the tenth day of this month each man is to take a lamb for his family, one for each household. If any household is too small for a whole lamb, they must share one with their nearest neighbour, having taken into account the number of people there are.*

> *You are to determine the amount of lamb needed in accordance with what each person will eat. The animals you choose must be year old males* **without defect,** *and you may take them from the sheep or the goats. Take care of them until the fourteenth day of the month, when all the*

people of the community of Israel must slaughter them at twilight.

Then they are to take some of the blood and put it on the sides and tops of the door-frames of the houses where they eat the lambs. That same night they are to eat the meat roasted over the fire, along with bitter herbs and bread made without yeast. **Do not eat the meat raw or cooked in water but roast it over the fire,** *head, legs and inner parts. Do not leave any of it till morning; if some is left till morning you must bum it.*

This is how you are to eat: with your cloak tucked into your belt, your sandals on your feet your staff in your hand. Eat it in haste; it is the Lord's Passover. On that same night I will pass through Egypt and strike down every first born - both men and animals - and I will bring judgement on all the gods of Egypt.

I am the Lord. The blood will be a sign for you on the houses where you are; and when I see the blood, I will pass-over you. No destructive plague will touch you when I strike Egypt.

The Whole Community and none Excluded

Notice in the third verse it says, *"...tell the whole community of Israel that each man has to take a lamb for his family and his household."* **Whole community** implies that God wants to reach all, for the scriptures tell us that Jesus was the reconciliation of the whole world, *(Romans 11:15),* every single person, man, woman, and child, regardless of colour.

This Passover was God's protection and provision for His people. The blood that was sprinkled upon the doorposts was for protection, a sign for deliverance not only from death, but also from the slavery of Egypt. One thing that we can be sure of as Christians is that we are in the world but not of it *(2 Corinthians 10:3)*.

We have been set free from being enslaved to the world, through the overcoming Christ *(Romans 12:2)*. The bitter herbs remind us of the suffering that we went through in the world. As long as we stay under the protection of the blood, for we have been washed in His blood *(Hebrews 9:14)*, we can remain free from sickness and disease that so often can afflict.

For when Satan sees the blood of Christ, there is no way that he is able to inflict, for scripture says no destructive plague will touch you. Jesus stripped the enemy and having disarmed the powers and authorities, he made a public spectacle of them, triumphing over them by the cross *(Colossians 2:15)*.

When Christ came as High Priest of the good things that are already here, he went through the greater and more perfect tabernacle that is not man made, that is to say, not a part of this creation. He did not enter by means of the blood of goats and calves; but he entered the most Holy Place once and for all by his own blood, having obtained eternal redemption.

Offered Himself

The blood of goats and bulls and the ashes of a heifer sprinkled on those who are ceremonially unclean sanctified them so that they are outwardly clean. How much more, then, will the blood of Christ, who through the eternal Spirit offered himself unblemished to God, cleanse our consciences from acts that led to death so that we may serve the living God! *(Hebrews 9:11-14)*

For this reason we know that Christ became the New Covenant that we might receive an eternal inheritance. He was the only ransom, which could be given to set us free.

For when Christ came into the world He said,

> *Sacrifice and offering you did not desire, but a body you prepared for me; with burnt offerings and sin offerings you were not pleased. Then I said, "here I am - it is written about me in the scroll - I have come to do your will - O God."*
>
> *(Hebrews 10:5-7)*

By one sacrifice He has made perfect forever those who are being made holy. The Holy Spirit also testifies to us about this.

> *This is the covenant I will make with them after that time, says the Lord, I will put my laws in their hearts, and I will write them on their minds.*
>
> *(Hebrews 10:16)*

Living Victorious Over Satan

The blood that Jesus shed for us cleanses us from every sin as long as we confess them to God and receive forgiveness *(1 John 1:7-9)*. If we live under the protection of the blood of Jesus, Satan is unable to get a foothold within our lives *(Ephesians 4:27)*. We as believers must know where we stand in God. **The blood of Jesus enables us to live victoriously over Satan** *(Revelations 12:11)*.

The blood of Jesus, the shedding of His blood and Him not once failing in one of the smallest details, resulted in the defeat of Satan and the cancelling out all of his claims upon the entire human race.

Satan is defeated by the blood of the Lamb, so through the blood of Jesus we are:

- Cleansed from sin and forgiven *(1 John 1:9)*
- Justified *(1 Corinthians 6:11)*
- Given access into His presence *(Ephesians 2:18)*
- Sanctified, and made holy *(1 Corinthians 6:11)*
- Given victory over Satan *(1 Corinthians 15:57)*
- Redeemed *(Ephesians 1:7)*

Piercing the Darkness

Music is the most powerful force on the earth, scientifically light travels at approximately 186,000 miles per second, travelling at such a high speed that it carries a threshold of audio-ability *(sound being music or song)*.

The bible tells us:

You are all sons of the light...
(1 Thessalonians 5:5)

God is light and in Him there is no darkness, our worship unto Him is light.

What we see with our human visibility is supposedly only 3% of the light spectrum. Now if God were to readjust the scope of our human visibility, from 3% to 40% of the light spectrum, we would actually be able to see our own worship *(projecting burning light!)*

Consider! As we worship God, our power filled praise and worship confronts the darkness all around us in the atmosphere, *(the principalities and the powers of the air)*. In other words, anointed worship helps to cleanse the atmosphere - dispelling and driving the darkness back.

This kind of effective worship, along with the faithful preaching of God's Word and faithful intercession - this is how *"open heavens"* can be created and entire regions impacted for Christ. Because every opposing force is successfully pushed back so that genuine spiritual freedom is felt and enjoyed by everyone.

> *When the righteous are in authority, the people rejoice: but when the wicked beareth rule, the people mourn.*
>
> *(Proverbs 29:2 KJV)*

> *I will declare your name to my brothers; in the congregation I will praise you.*
>
> *(Psalm 22:22)*

> *Save me from all the power of the enemy, from this roaring lion raging against me and the power of his dark*

horde. I will praise your name before all my brothers; as my people gather I will praise you in their midst.

(Psalm 22:21-22 TPT)[1]

So every time we worship God, Jesus comes in our midst and begins to praise His Father, and as we worship the Lord, God not only hears our praises but **He sees them also!**

As we are worshipping God, our worship dispels *(scatters)* the kingdom of darkness. As sons and daughters of light *(1 Thessalonians 5:5)* we are worshipping the Father of Lights, and that worship defeats Satan.

So often we forget as Christians that God is ready and willing to put into motion the heavenly host, to war against the hosts of evil. There are many passages in scripture, which show that the un-fallen angels have a ministry of war for the saints here on earth.

Are not all angels ministering spirits sent to those who will inherit salvation?

(Hebrews 1:14)

In the book of Revelations chapter twelve, Michael and his angels are seen fighting against the dragon and his angels. The united forces of the angelic hosts and the church are together in this battle and again we see the ministry of angels on behalf of the saints in Daniel 10 where Michael the Archangel resists the interference of the satanic prince of Persia.

More than Enough Angelic Protection

Our Lord Jesus referred also to the legions of angels He could have called to His aid to protect and deliver Him during the hour of power and darkness:

Do you suppose that I cannot appeal to My Father, and He will immediately provide Me with more than twelve legions [more than 80,000] of angels?
(Matthew 26:53 AMPC)

Don't you realize that I could ask my heavenly Father for angels to come at any time to deliver me? And instantly he would answer me by sending twelve armies of the angelic host to come and protect us.
(Matthew 26:53 TPT)[2]

Either way, whether it was more than 70,000 or over 80,000, the basic point is that the number of angels at Christ's immediate disposal would have been **more than enough!**

Yet Jesus chose to fight the battle through alone, accepting no heavenly rescue; though He did except some angelic assistance and ministry at other times, for example the angels that gathered to strengthen Him in the desert *(Matthew 4:11)* or the angel sent to strengthen Him so He could continue praying, in the garden of Gethsemane *(Luke 22:43)*.

Peter's Example

We know through scripture that God is also willing to send angelic help for us too, in our hours of need. For an example, let's look at Peter's miraculous escape from prison in Acts 2:1-17.

So Peter was kept in prison, but the church was earnestly praying to God for him. The night before Herod intended to bring him to trial, Peter was sleeping between two soldiers, bound with two chains, and sentries stood guard at the entrance.

Suddenly an angel of the Lord appeared and a light shone in the cell. He struck Peter on the side and woke him up. *"Quick get up!"* he said, and the chains fell off Peter's wrists. Then the angel said to him, *"Put on your clothes and sandals."* And Peter did so. *"Wrap your cloak around you and follow me,"* the angel told him.

Peter followed him out of the prison, but he had no idea what the angel was doing, or what was really happening; he thought he was seeing a vision or having a dream! They passed the first and second guards and came to the Iron Gate leading to the city. It opened for them by itself!

Comical Disbelief

People in the Jerusalem church were gathered praying for Peter's release. Meanwhile *(v13)* Peter knocked at the outer entrance, the servant girl came and answered the door. Once she recognized Peter's voice, she was so overjoyed she ran back without opening the door and exclaimed, *"Peter's at the door!"* And then what did the gathered church say? *"You're out of your mind woman!"*

That's so very typical. Very often, we don't even believe our own prayers! If God sent an angel, at midnight to our own front door, would we behave any differently?

Our Assurance in Battle:

- All is placed under our feet *(Ephesians 1:21-23)*

- Jesus has given us His authority *(Matthew 10:1)*

- He that's in us, is greater than he that's in the world *(1 John 4:4)*

- There's power in the blood of Jesus *(Revelation 12:11)*

Paul urged, ***"be strong in the Lord,"*** referring to the fact that we must rely on God's strength and not on our own.

Boldness not Timidity

We must be bold if we want to walk in victory. We are soldiers in the army of the Lord, and if we think in the context of spiritual *militancy* – we could refer this to the cultivation of a warrior spirit and proactive attitude; opposed to a passive and unwilling spirit.

In this context, as believers we have every reason to be bold and *militant,* as winners not losers, as the head and not the tail.

Like soldiers, believers have to start thinking in terms of "offence rather than just defence," simply because the church is going to have to stand and fight the devil every inch of the way.

The accuser of the brethren is doing his job day and night. His slander is relentless, *"…the accuser of our brethren, he who keeps bringing before our God charges against them day and night" (Revelation 12:10 AMPC).* Yet there seems to be too many laid-back Christians.

I suggest that spiritually lazy, horizontal and laid-back Christians don't need armour but a soft pillow! In reality believers need to wake up and smell the coffee. There is a spiritual battle raging, all around us and we must not be delinquent. The next generation will inherit what we failed to achieve.

❖

Chapter 2

Correct Posturing

Jesus called in a Loud Voice

It's time to go beyond defensive posturing and put on the whole armour of God to become holy warriors, alert - ready and on the offense! It's time to rise up, against the enemy of our souls and of the cross but never against flesh and blood.

I must clarify, that while using words like *warrior* this in no way suggests that we should be some variation between *religious nuts* or *violent zealots*. No! Rather our posturing towards people should always be gentle, fair and without aggression - like doves:

Remember, it is I who sends you out, even though you feel vulnerable as lambs going into a pack of wolves. So be as

*shrewd as snakes yet as harmless **as doves.***
(Matthew 10:16 TPT)

*Behold, I am sending you out like sheep in the midst of wolves; be wary and **wise as serpents,** and be innocent (harmless, guileless, and without falsity) as doves.*
(Matthew 10:16 AMPC)

To further cement any notions of balance here, let's add that while doves are seen as innocent and non-aggressive, we still must not be ignorant of Satan's devices or be stupidly naïve *(concerning evil men and evil intentions).* Equally no! We must be *wise as serpents* and permanently **on guard** like watchmen on the walls, possessing wisdom, strength and discernment:

*****Be on guard against men*** [whose way or nature is to act in opposition to God]; for they will deliver you up to councils and flog you in their synagogues...*
(Matthew 10:17 AMPC)

Holy Boldness is not Oblivious or ill Informed

Satan is trying to bring all sorts of corruption, not just into the world but also into the church. So it's time to submit to God, resist the devil and watch him flee! It's time to strategize with the Holy Spirit and know what He's doing in the land and within the regions where we live.

For example we do not always have to pray on our knees, we can walk around, we can run, we can jump, we can dance, and we can wave our arms around. We need to pray boldly, and that often but not always, involves praying with some volume! *"The Righteous are as Bold as a Lion"* (Proverbs 28:1).

For example a lion roars loudly, not softly! When he roars he roars. So when we are looking to function in boldness, we can't be afraid of the sound of our own voices. In fact, on numerous occasions in scripture Jesus can be seen, "crying out in a loud voice." On one obvious occasion, in John 11:43 *"Jesus called in a **loud voice,** 'Lazarus, come out!'"*

Though He's the Lion of the tribe of Judah, this doesn't mean that Jesus went about shouting all the time, no more than any lion roars all the time. But when it's time to roar, they don't hold back!

Finding our Roar

We've got to locate our own roar of faith, and never hold back when it's time. There's a time for whispering and a time for shouting. If your child was snatched before you, you certainly wouldn't just politely whisper, *"Oh dearest kidnapper, please don't be so cruel!"* No, you'd abandon all restraint and yell at the top your voice ***"STOP!"***

Remember, *"The thief comes only to steal and kill and destroy… (John 10:10)* The word only, suggests that our enemy has no other interest than explicitly: stealing, killing and destroying and is hell-bent on those three main objectives.

So we better learn to shout with authority - revealing who we are in Christ Jesus - Satan has to flee. He has no other option.

We have every right to be bold as we already have the victory in Jesus. Satan should never be running *after* us but running *from* us because we are more than conquerors.

The sting of death is sin, and the power of sin is the law. But thanks be to God! **He gives us the victory through our Lord Jesus Christ.**

(1 Corinthians 15:56-57)

Who shall separate us from the love of Christ? Shall trouble or hardship or persecution or famine or nakedness or danger or sword? As it is written: "For your sake we face death all day long; we are considered as sheep to be slaughtered." **No, in all these things we are more than conquerors through him who loved us.**

(Romans 8:35-37)

We must learn to operate in holy boldness as we are instructed in Acts:

Now, Lord, consider their threats and enable your servants to speak your word with **great boldness.**

(Acts 4:29)

Not Timid

New Testament Christians were not weak and wimpy; they were strong and enduring. Persecutions would not hinder their vision in any way. John the Baptist came boldly proclaiming to king Herod and the chief priests: Repent! For the Kingdom of God is at hand.

His words were not filled with wimpy religious phrases. His message was clear, bold, blasting and to the point. He gave the Word of God boldly. The message in New Testament times was the same to all, to the powerful, the weak, the rich, the poor, the famous and the unknown, and it must be the same today. It should not matter what town or what church we are part of, the message should be the same.

Boldness needs to come back into the church and the fear of retaliation must leave. We need God pleasers and not man pleasers; men and women who will boldly preach the Word of the Lord, without compromise or losing position. We need boldness to proclaim that our faith in God works.

Boldness to Overcome in Three Specific Realms

*What I'm going through has actually caused many believers to become even more courageous in the Lord and to be **bold and passionate** to preach the Word of God, all because of my chains.*

(Philippians 1:14 TPT)

We've been equipped with holy boldness for good reason. Let me just say, that after decades of experience dealing with all three of these realms, you'll be unequivocal about being timid!

The Heavenly Realm:

*In whom we have **boldness and access with confidence** through faith in Him.*

(Ephesians 3:12 NKJV)

*Now we are brothers and sisters in God's family because of the blood of Jesus, and he welcomes us to come right into the most holy sanctuary **in the heavenly realm— boldly and with no hesitation.***

(Hebrews 10:19 TPT)

*Let us therefore **come boldly** to the throne of grace, that we may obtain mercy and find grace to help in time of need.*

(Hebrews 4:16 NKJV)

The Earthly Realm:

*Please pray for me. Pray that truth will be with me before I even open my mouth. Ask the Spirit to guide me while I **boldly defend** the mystery that is the good news...*

(Ephesians 6:19 VOICE)

We are to be bold here on earth to boldly proclaim the gospel of Jesus Christ to the people of the world. We must boldly use the name of Jesus, proclaiming the truth and that Jesus has the power and authority to meet every need.

Word of warning: When the gospel of Jesus Christ is preached boldly and without restriction, religious people get disturbed and convicted!

The Demonic Realm:

The authority of the name of Jesus** causes every knee to bow in reverence! Everything and everyone will one day submit to this name – **in the <u>heavenly realm</u>, in the <u>earthly realm</u>, and in the <u>demonic realm</u>.

(Philippians 2:10 TPT)

According to the footnote for verse 11, *"God decreed that everyone in heaven will bow in worship of the God-Man... **that every demonic being will bow to the God-Man."***

With this knowledge we must stand and boldly put to flight demonic forces in the name of Jesus. Many believers do not know how to be bold when it comes to dealing with certain situations. They do not know how to enforce victory or declare authority over evil forces, in Christ's name.

As believers we need to know precisely who we are in Christ, possessing enough confidence in Him, to stand boldly against all forms of opposition. Living on the offence rather than defence, means that **we don't always run *from* battle.**

The Battle belongs to the Lord

Remember, as much as we are engaged in spiritual combat, the ultimate battle still belongs to the Lord. Remember how David face planted Goliath using one small stone because He doesn't "*...depend on weapons to fulfil his plans — he works without regard to human means!*" *(1 Samuel 17:47 TLB)*

Goliath gets Face Planted:

> *Then David said to the Philistine,* **"You come to me with a sword, a spear, and a javelin, but I come to you in the <u>name</u> of the Lord of hosts, the God of the armies of Israel, whom you have taunted.** *This day the Lord will hand you over to me, and I will strike you down and cut off your head.*
>
> *And I will give the corpses of the army of the Philistines this day to the birds of the sky and the wild beasts of the earth, so that all the earth may know that there is a God in Israel, and that this entire assembly may know that* **the**

Lord does not save with the sword or with the spear; for the battle is the <u>Lord's</u> and He will hand you over to us."

*When the Philistine rose and came forward to meet David, David ran quickly <u>toward</u> the battle line to meet the Philistine. David put his hand into his bag and took out a stone and slung it, and it struck the Philistine on his forehead. The stone penetrated his forehead, **and he fell <u>face down</u> on the ground.***

*So David triumphed over the Philistine with a sling and **a stone,** and he struck down the Philistine and killed him; **but there was no sword in David's hand. So he ran and stood over the Philistine, grasped his sword** and drew it out of its sheath and killed him, and cut off his head with it. When the Philistines saw that their [mighty] champion was dead, **they fled.***

(1 Samuel 17:45-49 AMP)

Notice how David required both the stone and the sword to fully defeat Goliath *(and make the rest of the army flee, James 4:7; Ephesians 6:17)*. **Today it still requires both the Rhema and the Logos in spiritual battle.** The sword of the Spirit represents the Rhema, the SPOKEN Word of God, which is released into the atmosphere via revelation knowledge from the Holy Spirit. And the written Word of God represents the Logos, *[eternal covenant / legal authority]*.

Notice too how David ran *towards* the battle rather than not *from* it, *(this is the mark of a happy warrior who believes in his mandate)*, because he didn't lack the courage of his convictions! If we use the Word of God *(both written and spoken)*, with equal audacity, our foe will also end up on its *face* or *fleeing with terror,* much the same way!

Fearless

We do not have to fear the devil or any of his works because we have victory in Jesus' name. We must also stop looking at our weaknesses and shortcomings and begin to realise that we are the *"righteousness of God in Christ"* *(2 Corinthians 5:21).*

We have the legal right to use the name of Jesus in the face of all manner of hostility. Even those that come ways we least expect:

> *Jesus turned to Peter and said,* **"Get out of my way, you Satan!** *You are an offense to me, because your thoughts are only filled with man's viewpoints and not with the ways of God."*
>
> *(Matthew 16:23 TPT)*

According to the footnotes for verse 23, *"Jesus is equating Peter's display of character to that of Satan. Peter was not possessed by Satan, but speaking from* **Satan's realm** *and speaking* **demonic wisdom..."**

> *This [superficial] wisdom is not that which comes down from above, but is earthly (secular), natural (unspiritual),* **even demonic.**
>
> *(James 3:15 AMP)*

Full of Courage

We too can be bold towards demons, sickness, disease, poverty and every evil work of the enemy, because of who we are in Christ and can boldly say: *"Satan has absolutely no authority over me, because he is already a defeated foe,"* *(see Matthew 18:18; Philippians 2:9-11; Colossians 2:15).*

We are not ridiculous ghost busters or animated dragon chasers. No! However it is guaranteed in this lifetime, *(whether we like it or not)* that we're going to encounter the demonic realm at some point or other and it can't be avoided.

"We are in this world but not of it" and without even trying we will attract demon's attention. They see the light of God on our lives and they fear us! They recognise those who truly walk with God, as Paul did and who carried the same anointing and authority as Jesus: *"The evil spirit retorted, 'I know and recognize and acknowledge Jesus, and I know about Paul, but as for you, who are you?'"* *(Acts 19:15 AMP)*

However, God has provided us with the necessary equipment to deal with demons. They were no problem to Jesus or to Paul, so should not be for us either. **The point is this, if demons know who we are in Christ, then we better know who we are!**

Enforcing Christ's Victory

In basic terms: **Demonic powers rule when godly people don't!** When they refuse to enforce the victory and the rightful spiritual dominion that the second Adam *[Christ]* restored. When they become stubbornly and progressively passive, in the face of the kind of opposition that they could easily overcome.

They rule when the people of God aren't willing to stand boldly and resist the powers of darkness through assertive prayer and with bold preaching, against sin and unrighteousness *(James 5:16)*.

We need to rise up. God wants prayer warriors, who know how to gain victories in all realms. Happy warriors run into battle, not for the sake of war but to fulfil their trained responsibilities.

For example on 9/11 the world watched as brave fire fighters ran into the twin towers, when everyone else was running away from them, in order to battle the flames.

Wrap-around God brings up the Rear

In addition, law enforcement officers around the globe are trained to run toward bullets, in order to protect innocent civilians and to fight crime.

Authority is another word for responsibility. No one runs towards bullets, battles and towering infernos without good reason! And as holy warriors in the army of the Lord, our battle is a spiritual one, which requires us to put out fires all the time, *(without behaving like rabbits caught in headlights)*.

We are brave, because we too believe in our heavenly mandate. We are trained, willing and able to do the Lord's bidding, conscious of His wrap-around presence and protection. ***"You are our King, the holiest one of all; your wrap-around presence is our protection"*** *(Psalm 89:18 TPT)*.

*His massive arms are wrapped around you,
protecting you. You can run under his covering of
majesty and hide. His arms of faithfulness are a shield
keeping you from harm.*

(Psalm 91:4 TPT)

*Go in confidence and grace – no rushing, no frantic
escape. There's no need to be anxious – the Eternal One
goes before and behind you. The God of Israel paves the
way with assurance and strength. **He watches your
back.***

(Isaiah 52:12 VOICE)

❖

CHAPTER 3

Authority to use His Name

Our Legal Rights in Christ

In the last chapter we touched on correct posturing, now I want to discuss the authority we have been given, in order to use that power. As warriors and new creation beings, we must realise that we have possession of the righteousness of God through Sonship, which gives us the legal authority to use His name, containing **"ALL AUTHORITY IN HEAVEN AND ON EARTH"** *(see Matthew 28:18-20).*

Through our union with Christ in heaven, we are legal heirs and carriers of this divine authority and it must be used, without delay on this earth. Consider! Such authority and power - all wrapped up in His name - given to us His church, here on earth.

Again, when Jesus said in Matthew 28:18 (KJV), *"All authority has been given unto me in heaven and on earth,"* He intended to give this to His new creation beings.

> *It is because of him that you are in Christ Jesus, who has become for us wisdom from God – that is, our righteousness, holiness and redemption.*
>
> *(1 Corinthians 1:30)*

> *So that no mortal man should [have pretense for glorying and] boast in the presence of God. But it is from Him that you have your life in Christ Jesus, Whom God made our Wisdom from God, [revealed to us a knowledge of the divine plan of salvation previously hidden, manifesting itself as] our* **Righteousness [thus making us upright and putting us in right standing with God]**, *and our Consecration [making us pure and holy], and our Redemption [providing our ransom from eternal penalty for sin].*
>
> *(1 Corinthians 1:29-30 AMPC)*

Impartation of Unlimited Righteousness

This righteousness makes a man actually one with Christ; made him creative, caused him to take authority *(enforce dominion spiritually)* and overcome in all of his circumstances, *(to rule and not be ruled)*.

> *This righteousness is given through faith in Jesus Christ to all who believe.*
>
> *(Romans 3:22)*

In the New Testament we posses unlimited righteousness, whereas in the Old Testament, righteousness was only reckoned *(tallied, calculated, transactional)* to God's people. *"It was not through the law that Abraham and his offspring received the promise that he would be heir of the world, but through the righteousness that comes by faith" (Romans 4:13).*

On the contrary, in the New Testament, righteousness is received by *impartation.* Given by the Father, through Christ, to man.

"God made him who had no sin to be sin for us, so that in him we might become the righteousness of God" (2 Corinthians 5:21). We have become righteous by the New Creation. This new and wonderful righteousness makes us fit companions of Jesus and will fit us for our eternal fellowship with the Father through the ages to come.

This is the brilliance and the mystery of redemption, the miracle of the New Creation. Consider! Dare we really think of ourselves just as the Father says we are? Dare we really go into His presence with fearless joy, making our requests known to Him?

Yes dear Child this really is your Father!

If we really knew who we were, life would be so different! We would talk of the miracles that were taking place daily.

Praise be to the God and Father of our Lord Jesus Christ, who has blessed us in the heavenly realms with every spiritual blessing in Christ. For he chose us in him before the creation of the world to be holy and blameless in his sight. In love he predestined us for adoption to sonship through Jesus Christ, in accordance with his pleasure and will - to the praise of his glorious grace, which he has freely given us in the One he loves.

In him we have redemption through his blood, the forgiveness of sins, in accordance with the riches of God's grace that he lavished on us.

With all wisdom and understanding, he made known to us the mystery of his will according to his good pleasure, which he purposed in Christ, to be put into effect when the times reach their fulfilment – to bring unity to all things in heaven and on earth under Christ.

In him we were also chosen, having been predestined according to the plan of him who works out everything in conformity with the purpose of his will.

(Ephesians 1:3-11)

In the name of the Jesus our Redeemer and King we have unlimited access into the Father's presence, at any time: *"Whatsoever you ask in my name I will give it to you" (John 14:13)*. We are not honouring our place as sons, or our standing in righteousness, unless we take our place. Let us make the Father, the Lord Jesus Christ and the Holy Spirit proud of us.

It is important to remember, Jesus was as much a human being as we are. He was a man in every sense of the word. If He were not He would not have been able to deal with the legal issue involved in the redemption work of the cross.

Consider still! Jesus said, that we would do even greater things than He.

I tell you the truth, anyone who has faith in me will do what I have been doing. He will do even greater things than these, because I am going to the Father. And I will do whatever you ask in my name, so that the Son may bring glory to the Father.

(John 14:12-13)

Authority in Action

It is said that Smith Wigglesworth brought at least 18 people back to life, raising them from the dead. What authority! You have to know who you really are in Christ to be able to stand a corpse up against the wall and command it to live in the name of Jesus.

Smith Wigglesworth was a trained plumber, but in 1907, when he was 48, his life pattern was dramatically changed as a result of the baptism in the Holy Spirit. From a relatively small, part-time pastorate in Bradford, England, he stepped into a worldwide evangelistic and healing ministry.

Many of the healings that God performed through Smith Wigglesworth are recorded in *Ever Increasing Faith.*[1]

Authority in action refers to the church; we too must take our rightful places, as Smith did, unafraid of the task ahead and stand in a position of authority, allowing our voices to be heard. Nor did Smith apologize for the move of God, Who's still looking for men and women today, who'll turn from being men pleasers to God pleasers, delivered from spirits of fear and religion.

Follow the Example of Christ

Jesus took authority over the natural realm *(i.e. calmed the storm Mark 4:35-42; fed the 5000 Matthew 14:14-21)*, but also healed the sick, cast out demons and raised the dead.

Some examples of Jesus miracles:

A man with leprosy came to him and begged him on his knees, "If you are willing, you can make me clean." Jesus was indignant. He reached out his hand and touched the man. "I am willing," he said. **"Be clean!"** *Immediately the leprosy left him and he was cleansed.*

(Mark 1:40-42)

Some men brought to him a paralyzed man, lying on a mat. When Jesus saw their faith, he said to the man, "Take heart, son; your sins are forgiven." At this, some of the teachers of the law said to themselves, "This fellow is blaspheming!" Knowing their thoughts, Jesus said, "Why do you entertain evil thoughts in your hearts? Which is easier: to say, Your sins are forgiven, or to say, Get up and walk? But I want you to know that the Son of Man **has authority on earth** *to forgive sins." So he said to the paralyzed man, "Get up, take your mat and go home." Then the man got up and went home.*

(Matthew 9:2-7)

While they were going out, a man who was demon-possessed and could not talk was brought to Jesus. And when **the demon was driven out,** *the man who had been mute spoke. The crowd was amazed and said, "Nothing like this has ever been seen in Israel."*

(Matthew 9:32-33)

*Then with a loud voice **Jesus shouted with authority:** "Lazarus! Come out of the tomb!" Then in front of everyone, Lazarus, who had died four days earlier, slowly hobbled out – he still had grave clothes tightly wrapped around his hands and feet and covering his face! Jesus said to them, "Unwrap him and let him loose."*

(John 11:43-44 TPT)

Roaring in His Authority

Roaring is a sign of the authority of the Lion of Judah, who lives, breathes, and dwells within us.

*As a hero throws himself into battle, the Eternal will take on His enemies; with passion, **shouting out a deafening roar, He will power over them.***

(Isaiah 42:13 VOICE)

*Yahweh goes out to battle like a hero and stirs up his passion and zeal **like a mighty warrior**...*

(Isaiah 42:13-14 TPT)

*The Lord will march out like a mighty man; like a warrior he will stir up His zeal; with a shout **he will raise the battle cry and will triumph over his enemies**...*

(Isaiah 42:13)

***He will signal to distant nations, and whistle for their armies: unleash the dogs of war.** At breakneck speed they come, a war machine like no other – Never tired, never weak; no one needs to rest or sleep. Not a belt needs tightening, not a sandal strap needs fixing. Their arrows have been sharpened; their bows have been bent,* *ready for action. Their horses' hooves spark like flint; their chariots' wheels spin like whirlwinds.*

Their roaring is deafening, like a lion, like a pack of roaring lions. *When they attack, they growl and pounce on their prey, carrying them away; no chance of a rescue. On that day,* ***they will roar over this people like a roaring, angry sea,*** *and the land will go sorrowfully dark, the light eclipsed by the clouds of war.*

(Isaiah 5:26-30 VOICE)

It's easy to read scripture and make random conclusions about the rights and wrongs of standing on certain truths, especially when it comes to Old versus New Testaments scriptures.

In this context, I want to draw our attention to Joel 2:28, which was the very prophesy Peter declared in Acts 2:17, and which we know came to pass on the day of Pentecost.

Then in those days I will pour My Spirit to all humanity; your children will boldly and prophetically speak the word of God. Your elders will dream dreams; ***your young warriors will see visions.***

(Joel 2:28 VOICE)

Rouse the Warriors!

However, if we read further in the book of Joel, another prophecy is declared, saying:

Proclaim this among the nations: ***Prepare for war! Rouse the warriors! Let all the fighting men draw*** *near and attack. Beat your plough shares into swords and your pruning hooks into spears. Let the weakling say "I am strong!" Come quickly all you nations from every side, and assemble there.*

Bring down your warriors, O Lord! "Let the nations be roused; let them advance into the Valley of Jehoshaphat, for there I will sit to judge all the nations on every side. Swing the sickle, for the harvest is ripe. Come, trample the grapes for the wine press is full and the vats overflow - so great is their wickedness!"

Multitudes, multitudes in the valley of decision! For the day of the Lord is near in the valley of decision. The sun and moon will be darkened, and stars no longer shine. The Lord will roar from Zion and thunder from Jerusalem; the earth and the sky will tremble. But the Lord will be a refuge for his people, a stronghold for the people of Israel.

(Joel 3:9-16)

Throwing off our Weaknesses

God so desires for us to throw off our weaknesses and take on a new stance, proclaiming that we are strong not weak: *"Let the weak one throw out his chest and say, 'I'm tough, I'm a fighter'"* (Joel 3:10 MSG).

This is an act of one's will, to be determined to stand and not to waver. Because it is only from this position, as we swing the sickle, that the harvest will be reaped.

Swing the sickle — the harvest is ready. Stomp on the grapes — the winepress is full. **The wine vats are full, overflowing with vintage evil.**
(Joel 3:13 MSG)

Joel said that the multitudes are in the valley of decision, an interesting thought: *"Multitudes, multitudes in the valley of decision! For the day of the Lord is near in the valley of decision"* (Joel 3:14).

Consider. Jesus also told His disciples in Matthew 9:37, *"Ask the Lord of the harvest... to send out* **workers** *into his* **harvest field."** Such workers aught first to be warriors, able to stomach the battlefield that is the harvest field. An arena that can be volatile indeed!

Mass confusion, <u>mob uproar</u> *— in Decision Valley! God's Judgment Day has arrived in Decision Valley.*
(Joel 3:14 MSG)

❖

CHAPTER 4

The Meaning of the Word Authority

The Lawful Right to Exercise Power

Authority (*greek-exousia*) - (*from the impersonal verb exesti, "it is lawful"*). From the meaning of, leave or permission, or ability or strength with which one is endued, then to that of the power of authority, **the right to exercise power.**[1]

Jesus, in John 17:1-5 prayed:

Father, the time has come. **Glorify your Son, that your son may glorify you.** *For you granted him authority, [the Aramaic is translated "responsibility"], over all people that he might give eternal life to all those you have given him.*

*Now this is eternal life: that they may know you, the only true God, and Jesus Christ, whom you have sent. I have brought you glory on earth by completing the work you gave me to do. And now, Father, glorify me in your presence with **the glory I had with you before the world began.***

These few verses remind me of the grace of God, His splendour and glory, and yet He gave this up for us, not to lord it over us but to come and serve us *(Philippians 2:6-11).* The realization or the revelation that God who is eternal and all-powerful and having absolute authority, gave up His position to come and save mankind is amazing!

Glory through Obedience

Jesus brought glory to the Father through His obedience. This is our purpose too, as we walk the path of obedience. **"Glorify your Son, that your Son may glorify you"** *(John 17:1).* Jesus is our perfect example; concerning this Spurgeon said:

> **The great design of Christ, throughout his life on earth, was to glorify the Father.** *He came to save his people, but that was not his first or his chief aim.* **It was his objective, through the salvation of myriads of the sons of men, to glorify the Father.**[2]

It's important to look at the points Jesus made in His Prayer:

- It was the Father who gave Jesus authority *[responsibility].* The Father gave Jesus authority to do the works of the Kingdom. This was the reason that He came *(John 5:26-27).*

54

- "For as the Father has life in himself, so he has granted the Son also to have life in himself. And he has given him authority to judge because he is the Son of Man" *(John 5:26-27).*

- "That everyone who believes may have eternal life in him" *(John 3:15).*

- His purpose was that the whole world might know the only true God. Bringing us back to the Father. This was the role of Jesus to bring us back, we the rebellious, the stiff-necked, as God often calls His people *(Exodus 32:9).*

Seven ways to have authority and reign in life:

- Decide to reign; you are born again with a new nature, so live it! *(Romans 6:14; Philippians 4:13)*
- Declare it *(Job 22:28; Romans 10:8-10; Mark 11:23-24)*
- Realize the Greater One is in you *(1 John 4:4)*
- Forget past failure *(1 John 1:9; Romans 8:1)*
- Be ready for battle *(Ephesians 6:10-12)*
- Forgive and get rid of strife *(Ephesians 4:25-26)*
- Praise God by faith *(Romans 4:17-22; Hebrews 13:15)*

The Sovereign Authority of Jesus

This authority, in the ministry of Jesus was recognised by others. One funny example is the seven sons of Sceva mentioned in Acts 19, *"One day the evil spirit answered them,*

'Jesus I know, and Paul I know about, but who are you?'" (Acts 19:15)

Equally though, we too must be recognised by His authority:

> Not everyone who says to me, "Lord, Lord," will enter the kingdom of heaven, but only the one who does the will of my Father who is in heaven.
>
> Many will say to me on that day, "Lord, Lord, did we not prophesy in your name and in your name drive out demons and in your name perform many miracles?" Then I will tell them plainly, **"I never knew you.** Away from me, you evildoers!"
>
> (Matthew 7:21-23)

Matthew 7:28-29 says: "*By the time Jesus finished speaking, the crowds were dazed and overwhelmed by his teaching, because* **his words carried such great authority,** *quite unlike their religious scholars*" (TPT).

Authority is delegated power. When Christ ascended, He transferred His authority to the church. He is the Head of the church, and believers make up the Body. The source of our authority is found in the resurrection:

> And having **disarmed the powers and authorities,** he made a public spectacle of them, triumphing over them by the cross.
>
> (Colossians 2:15)

Then Jesus made a public spectacle of all the powers and principalities of darkness, **stripping away from them every weapon and all their spiritual authority and power to accuse us.** *And by the power of the cross, Jesus led them around as prisoners in a procession of triumph.* **He was not their prisoner; they were his!**
(Colossians 2:15 TPT)

Sometimes I am saddened to hear men of God teaching from mere head knowledge, *(which exposes their gaping deficit of spiritual understanding).* This is because they don't know the authority that's rightfully theirs, as sons of God *(Ephesians 1:5).*

Spurgeon said, *"I wonder how long we might beat our brains before we could plainly put into word what is meant by preaching with unction. Yet he who preaches knows its presence, and he who hears soon detects its absence."*[3]

To be a leader or a teacher of the Word, we need to know how to stand in the authority that has been given through Christ *(Titus 2:15)*, then others will recognize our authority as a leader.

In conjunction with Spurgeon, E.M. Bounds offers this observation: *"Unction is simply putting God in his own word and on his own preachers."*

Unction is that indefinable, indescribable something which an old, renowned Scotch preacher describes thus: "There is sometimes somewhat in preaching that cannot be ascribed either to matter or expression, and cannot be described what it is, or from whence it cometh, but *with a **sweet violence it pierceth into the heart and affections and comes immediately from the Word** but if there be any way to obtain such a thing, it is by the heavenly disposition of the speaker."*[4]

The Anatomy of Authority

In the account of Matthew 8:5-13, the centurion saw in Jesus a quality that he recognized. He saw that when Jesus spoke, there was an even greater power working through Him – exceeding mere humanity. In fact what he saw was the transforming power of God working through Jesus:

When Jesus entered the village of Capernaum, a captain in the Roman army approached him, asking for a miracle. "Lord," he said, "I have a son who is lying in my home, paralyzed and suffering terribly." Jesus responded, "I will go with you and heal him."

*But the Roman officer interjected, "Lord, who am I to have you come into my house? **I understand your authority,** for I too am a man who walks under authority and have authority over soldiers who serve under me.*

I can tell one to go and he'll go, and another to come and he'll come. I order my servants and they'll do whatever I ask. So I know that all you need to do is to stand here and command healing over my son and he will be instantly healed."

Jesus was astonished when he heard this and said to those who were following him, "He has greater faith than anyone I've encountered in Israel...

Then Jesus turned to the Roman officer and said, "Go home. All that you have believed for will be done for you!" And his son was healed at that very moment.

So why did Jesus reckon such great faith to this Centurion, when at others times, He told others that they had little faith? The answer: **this Centurion understood the anatomy of authority, yet more importantly he recognised the authority of Christ** and openly acknowledged the authority behind Him.

We too need this calibre of faith, to recognise divine authority when we see it and realize that no one can function in any position of authority without first being under authority. In other words, all authority that exists without submission is illegitimate and unlawful *(and criminally enforced like the mafia for example!)*

Jesus at that time had not found anyone with such a clear understanding of His authority, because the centurion saw that Jesus was subject to an even greater authority. **All of Heaven was behind Him!**

This soldier spoke representing not his own authority, but the authority of Rome *(an empire spanning the known world at that time in history)*. The centurion saw an authority that he understood, which came from God. Equally so, when Jesus spoke, the whole power and authority of the Godhead was being represented through His words.

Jesus is the Word of God. In the beginning the Word was spoken and the earth came into being *(John 1:1)*. There was great power and authority coming from this man Jesus, whose voice brought healing at a distance, even the elements were obedient and life was subject to His command *(John 1:1-18; Colossians 1:15-20).*

E. W. Kenyon says, "The earth walk of the man *(Jesus)* reveals the fact that Israel had Jehovah on their hands. He was the One who was the author of the covenant, the law, the sacrifices, the One who had appointed the priesthood and the great day of atonement, **was in their midst and they did not recognize Him..."**

He goes on to say, "The tragedy of the garden scene, where the angels strengthened and comforted the rejected Jehovah the incarnate Son of God. The trial with its bitter jealousy, its deception and dishonesty, where the God of the Old Covenant was spat upon, reviled and cast out by the very people He had brought into being. The cross with its agonies, where the hero God-man became sin...

Perhaps the strangest feature of it all was that **not one person knew that He was dying for their sins,** that He was bearing the penalty of their transgressions."

The Authority of the Resurrection

Three days of gloom and darkness settled over the hearts of the disciples, their Kingdom dreams were ended:

As for you, you were dead in your transgressions and sins, in which you used to live when you followed the ways of this world and of the ruler of the kingdom of the air, the spirit who is now at work in those who are disobedient.

60

*All of us also lived among them at one time, gratifying the cravings of our flesh and following its desires and thoughts. Like the rest, we were by nature deserving of wrath. But because of his great love for us, God, who is rich in mercy, made us alive with Christ even when we were dead in transgressions - **it is by grace you have been saved.***

*And God raised us up with Christ and seated us with him in the heavenly realms in Christ Jesus, in order that in the coming ages he might show the incomparable riches of his grace, expressed in his kindness to us in Christ Jesus. **For it is by grace you have been saved, through faith - and this is not from yourselves, it is the gift of God** - not by works, so that no one can boast. For we are God's handiwork, created in Christ Jesus to do good works, which God prepared in advance for us to do.*

(Ephesians 2:1-10)

They didn't understand where the master had gone or what He was suffering. They were overwhelmed by His resurrection and mystified by the forty days prior to His ascension. Nor did they know that He had carried His blood into the heavenly Holy of Holies.

Little did they appreciate the fact that the cloud, which received Him out of their sight, consisted of Old Testament saints, being taken to the Father's House!

That He was to sit down at the right hand of the Majesty on High in the ultimate position of authority *(and that we were destined to be seated with Him there)*, they did not know. Nor did they realise that once the legal part of redemption had been accomplished, it would make way for crucial events in the upper room.

Even when they had watched Him hanging on a tree, they still didn't grasp the fact that Jesus was indeed Jehovah, the God of Abraham, Isaac and Jacob:

> *Those who passed by hurled insults at him, shaking their heads and saying, "You who are going to destroy the temple and build it in three days, save yourself! Come down from the cross, if you are the Son of God!"* **In the same way the chief priests, the teachers of the law and the elders mocked him. "He saved others," they said, "but he can't save himself!** *He's the king of Israel! Let him come down now from the cross, and we will believe in him. He trusts in God. Let God rescue him now if he wants him, for he said,* **'I am the Son of God.'"**
> (Matthew 27:39-43)

Israel was literally crucifying the blood covenant partner of Abraham and they were utterly blind to it!

In addition, when Jesus commanded His disciples, to wait until the Spirit came, they still had little comprehension of what was due to transpire. Here they were after following the miracle-man, yet they remained totally dull as to His true identity, purpose and suffering, including what they stood to gain from His agony.

All that has gone before us in the redemption work of Christ brings: justification, righteousness - the ability to stand in the presence of God - adoption and legal sonship. Our absolute legal right to stand justified, sanctified *(one in Christ)* before the Father, just as if we'd never sinned!

> *He that supplieth seed to the sower and bread for food, shall supply and multiply your seed for sowing, and* **increase the fruits of your righteousness.**
> (2 Corinthians 9:10 KJV)

Jesus said, *"I am the vine, and ye are the branches"* *(John 15:5 KJV)*. The vine is righteous and the branch is the righteousness of the vine. So the fruits that the vine would naturally bear through the branches will be called the fruits of righteousness. Those fruits will be the same type of fruit that Jesus bore in His earthly ministry.

We have the joy of bearing a type of fruit that Jesus could not bear in His earthly walk. Yes He could heal the sick, feed the hungry and raise the dead, but we bear another kind of fruit. We lead men *to* Christ, which brings them into eternal life!

We can lead them into the depth of the knowledge of God's righteousness, which He fashioned in Christ for them. We can do things for people's spirits that Christ could not do, as He had not yet died or paid sin's penalty, making the new creation possible.

Still, we can have this spiritual fruit in Christ, because being established in righteousness gives us a foundation on which to stand and an assurance in this life.

Masters not Slaves

Man has always been a servant of the devil; literal slaves to sin. But this is no longer true for the new-creation child of God:

> *Now, if anyone is enfolded into Christ, he has become an* **entirely new creation.** *All that is related to the old order has vanished. Behold, everything is fresh and new.*
> *(2 Corinthians 5:17 TPT)*

According to the footnotes for this particular verse, "This would include our old identity, our life of sin, the power of Satan, the religious works of trying to please God, our old relationship with the world, and our old mind-sets. **We are not reformed or simply refurbished, we are made completely new by our union with Christ and the indwelling of the Holy Spirit.**

> *I have been crucified with Christ and* **I no longer live,** *but Christ lives in me. The life I now live in the body, I live by faith in the Son of God, who loved me and gave himself for me.*
> *(Galatians 2:20)*

> *Thanks be to God that, though you* **used to be** *slaves to* **sin,** *you have come to obey from your heart the pattern of teaching that has now claimed your allegiance.*
> *(Romans 6:17)*

> *Thank God that* **your slavery to sin has ended** *and that in your new freedom you pledged your heartfelt obedience to that teaching which was passed on to you.*
> *(Romans 6:17 VOICE)*

As new creations, *(imparted with God's righteousness)*, we are the masters and no longer the slaves; no longer subjects of sin or the devil. We are no longer constantly talking of our weaknesses and failures, but rejoice in our newfound abilities to make the heart of the Father glad.

Only we must now act as though we know that we're righteous. Taking advantage of the fact that we are the righteousness of God. *"God made him who had no sin to be sin for us, so that in him we might become **the righteousness of God"** (2 Corinthians 5:21).*

> *He orchestrated this: the Anointed One, who had never experienced sin, became sin for us so that in Him we might **embody the very righteousness of God.***
> *(2 Corinthians 5:21 VOICE)*

We have a standing invitation to come into the throne room and visit with the Father at any time. Hebrews 4:16, ***"Come boldly unto the throne of grace."*** However we must be fully persuaded and convinced of who we are now, the very righteousness of God!

Just as any young bride realises *(once she is married)* that she is now the woman of the house; legal spouse to her husband. The two have become one!

❖

CHAPTER 5

Authority for Warfare

Trained for Battle

To stand and to operate in the authority of Christ means that we have to take on the weapons of our warfare. God's divine armoury is open to us for the destruction of the devil's kingdom, for king David wrote within the Psalms, *"blessed be the Lord my rock, who **trains my hands for war, and my fingers for battle"** (Psalm 144:1 NKJV).*

> *The Lord has opened His armoury, and has brought out the weapons of His indignation; for this is the word of the Lord God of hosts...*
>
> *(Jeremiah 50:25 NKJV)*

You are my battleaxe and weapons of war: for with you I will break the nations in pieces; with you I will destroy kingdoms.

(Jeremiah 51:20 NKJV)

It seems to me that spirits of witchcraft and religion, like to control what happens through the church. They have fought and continue to fight against the anointing that is upon God's men and women. **But God and those who are obedient to His call cannot be controlled,** they will either work according to His will or it won't work at all.

Take a minute to compare what three different bible translations say about the following same bible verses:

*For though we live in the world, we do not wage war as the world does. The weapons we fight with are not the weapons of the world. On the contrary, they have **divine power to demolish strongholds.***

*We demolish arguments and every pretension that sets itself up against the knowledge of God, and we **take captive every thought** to make it obedient to Christ.*

(2 Corinthians 10:3-5)

For although we live in the natural realm, we don't wage a military campaign employing human weapons, using manipulation to achieve our aims. Instead our spiritual weapons are energized with divine power to effectively dismantle the defences behind which people hide.[1]

We can demolish every deceptive fantasy that opposes God and break through every arrogant attitude that is raised up in defiance of the true knowledge of God. We capture, like prisoners of war, every thought[2] and insist that it bow in obedience to the Anointed One.

(2 Corinthians 10:3-5 TPT)

*The world is unprincipled. It's dog-eat-dog out there! The world doesn't fight fair. But we don't live or fight our battles that way — never have and never will. **The tools of our trade aren't for marketing or manipulation, but they are for demolishing that entire massively corrupt culture.***

We use our powerful God-tools for smashing warped philosophies, tearing down barriers erected against the truth of God, fitting every loose thought and emotion and impulse into the structure of life shaped by Christ. *Our tools are ready at hand for clearing the ground of every obstruction and building lives of obedience into maturity.*

(2 Corinthians 10:3-6 MSG)

The Price of Authority

I am not looking for persecution, but we know that scripture makes it clear in 2 Timothy 3:12, *"Everyone who wants to live a godly life in Christ Jesus will be persecuted."* Or as the Message bible bluntly puts it: *"Anyone who wants to live all out for Christ is in for a lot of trouble; there's no getting around it."*

We need to develop a strength and stamina in God, and stand and endure in His strength. The only concern or worry about what man might do or say, is our reaction to it.

God is preparing a glorious church without spot wrinkle or blemish, a church that has been prepared from the foundations of the world. A church that has been purged and cleansed; a church that is blameless, holy and walking in victory and **above all, a church that knows and lives in its divinely given authority.**

For without authority being in operation within our lives, how can we deal with powers and demonic spirits, spirits of the Anti-Christ, controlling spirits, lawlessness, and mammon; these must be broken over our cities and nations.

This is why there was an emphasis in the nineties, where God was saying to the church: *"Take your place, assume your rank, and come into your rightful position, so you can do what I have called you to do"* (this still applies).

Yes we will be persecuted for what we believe, but we mustn't live in fear of persecution. For every time persecution comes to the church, it only grows stronger! Like a diamond in the rough, it flourishes under pressure.

The early believers weren't wimps rather they developed strength and endurance and persecution didn't shake them from their vision of God. Equally then, through pressure our hearts and characters will be developed also.

Either persecution will cause us to be released into a new realm of the Spirit, where we'll receive a divine impartation that'll cause us to become new men and women in Christ. Or we'll allow fear and unbelief to drive us away from the very presence and stature of God, where the word *authority* will just be a word.

The Authority of Jesus

For Jesus, a life of ministering in authority began when He rejected the *authority* and *glory* of the kingdoms of this world. This being the temptation in Luke 4:6, where He was led into the wilderness by the Holy Spirit, and where Satan offered Him everything His eyes could see. **Similarly, if we don't reject the things of this world, we won't have authority over them!**

Satan said,

> *I will give you all their authority and splendor, for it has been given to me, and I can give it to anyone I want to. So if you worship me, it will all be yours.*
>
> (Luke 4:6-7)

> *For the second test he led him up and spread out all the kingdoms of the earth on display at once. Then the Devil said, "They're yours in all their splendor to serve your pleasure. I'm in charge of them all and can turn them over to whomever I wish. Worship me and they're yours, the whole works."*
>
> (Luke 4:6-7 MSG)

The flip side was true! If Jesus had accepted, then He would have traded a much higher authority for a lesser one, which was exactly Satan's ruse. Equally then, we must not mistake what's being offered to us by the devil, as something being offered by God.

No Trading Places

Jesus rejected this temptation to trade with Satan and lost zero authority, as we see later on in verse 36, after Jesus expelled a demon, all the people were amazed and said to one another, *"What is this teaching?* **With authority and power He gives orders to evil spirits and they come out!"**

So, Jesus had to choose between two different sources of authority. He turned His back on the idea of ruling through meagre political authority, knowing that His right to *(limitless)* rule came NOT from political force, but from the Most High God:

> *For as the Father has life in himself, so he has granted the Son to have life in himself. And* **he has given him authority** *to judge because he is the Son of Man.*
> *(John 5:26-27)*

When Jesus walked in Israel more than 2000 years ago, the Jewish nation was looking for a Messiah to come and conquer the Roman Empire, and take over as their king. But again, Jesus chose not to come and conquer the kingdoms of this world by civil war but to conquer the spiritual domain of Satan, *"this dark world" (Ephesians 6:11-12).*

The Apostle Paul states in Colossians, where and how the battle was won,

> *And having disarmed the powers and authorities, he made a public spectacle of them, triumphing over them by the Cross.*
> *(Colossians 2:15)*

Remembering,

> *The reason the Son of God appeared was to destroy the devil's work.*
>
> *(1 John 3:8)*

Moving under Authority

Jesus said, *"The Father ...has granted the son ...authority to execute Judgement" (John 5:26).*

As we look to the Father and as He speaks and shows us the way, and as we stand in the authority that we have been given, then we can move out in the authority that God has given us. This in turn will cause us to become fruitful within our lives and ministries.

> *By myself I can do nothing; I judge only as I hear, and my judgement is just, for I seek not to please myself but him who sent me.*
>
> *(John 5:30)*

Authority to Execute Judgement

John Wesley *(founder of the Methodist movement)* who travelled around on horseback preaching from village to village in 18th century Britain knew his authority in Christ. If people within a village did not respond to the message, he used to literally shake the dust off his feet, executing the judgement of Jesus Christ.

This is the very authority that we as believers have and should be moving in today:

Whatever village or town you enter, search for a godly man who will let you into his home until you leave for the next town. Once you enter a house, speak to the family there and say, **"God's blessing of peace be upon this house!"**

And if those living there welcome you, let your peace come upon the house. **But if you are rejected, that blessing of peace will come back upon you.**

And if anyone doesn't listen to you and rejects your message, when you leave that house or town, **shake the dust off your feet as a prophetic act that you will not take their <u>defilement</u> with you.***

Mark my words, on the day of judgment the wicked people who lived in the land of Sodom and Gomorrah will have a lesser degree of judgment than the city that rejects you, for the people of Sodom and Gomorrah did not have the opportunity that was given to them!

(Matthew 10:11-15 TPT)

However, according to the Passion Translation's footnotes for verse 14 it says, "Implied in the historical context of shaking dust off of one's feet when leaving a city. The 'uncleanness' [*defilement*] could also refer to any bitter response to the rejection they experienced. <u>They were to 'shake it off' before they went to their next assignment.</u>"

Authority without Mercy is Doomed

I like this because as believers and children of God, we are meant to walk in love and forgiveness, otherwise our testimony is critically flawed. For example, if we take one bitter experience of rejection *(persecution)* into another, it will cloud our judgment or poison our effectiveness.

Which reminds me of the incident with the Samaritan village where Jesus said to His disciples, ***"the Son of Man did not come to destroy men's lives but to save them."***

> *"Lord, do You want us to command fire to come down from heaven and consume them, just as Elijah did?" But He turned and rebuked them, and said, **"You do not know what manner of spirit you are of.** For the Son of Man did not come to destroy men's lives but to save them." And they went to another village.*
>
> *(Luke 9:53-57 NKJV)*

The Wycliffe Bible says it like this, "He turned, and blamed them, and said, ye know not, whose spirit ye be; for man's Son came not to destroy men's souls *[to lose men's souls]*, but to save *[them]*."

Mercy Triumphs over Judgment

Jesus showcased His mercy here, in that just one chapter on, He was seen teaching the parable of the Good Samaritan *(Luke 10:25-37)*. An entire Samaritan town received Jesus, due to the testimony of just one woman. Then later still, as mentioned in the book of Acts, an entire region of Samaritans *("many Samaritan villages" v25)*, received the good news of the gospel and entered the kingdom of God *(John 4:39-42; Acts 8:9-25)*.

Basically Jesus saw their redemptive future and what was to transpire for the Samaritans. Let me stress, God's love is always redemptive and it's good to remember, *(especially when discussing a subject like authority)*. The bible teaches, *"mercy triumphs over judgment."*

> *Speak and act as those who are going to be **judged by the law that gives freedom,** because judgment without mercy will be shown to anyone who has not been merciful. **Mercy triumphs over judgment.***
>
> *(James 2:12-13)*

> *So we must both speak and act in every respect like those who are destined to be tried by the perfect law of liberty, and remember that judgment is merciless for the one who judges others without mercy. **So by showing mercy you take dominion over judgment!***
>
> *(James 2:12-13 TPT)*

Or as the Wycliffe says, *...mercy rises above doom!* *(James 2:13 WYC)*

Consider Satan who comes to steal, kill and destroy and has only bondage and doom within him. Jesus, on the other hand came only to give freedom and life, and with His unrivalled authority He still shows mercy. We must never forget this, so perhaps we should paraphrase James 2:13 as; **"doomed is any authority that shows no mercy."**

In other words, if we function in authority on any level, *(even just the believer's authority)*, we must show mercy to God's people, otherwise His Word has already judged us!

Samaritans - Loved by Jesus

There was racial tension in those days between Jews and Samaritans; the hatred between them was mutual. So they were the least likely to stop and help a Jew! In fact as a Jew, Jesus' attitude towards Samaritans was revolutionary!

According to a small excerpt taken from an article written on Oxford Biblical Studies Online:

"The common heritage of Jews and Samaritans combined with the history of friction and dissent adds to the piquancy of **Jesus' friendliness towards them** *(Luke 17:18; John 4:7)* **and the astonishing anti-racism of the parable of the Good Samaritan** *(Luke 10:33)."*[3]

To help us understand this better, let me also share some excerpts from my own material, Understanding the Political, Religious & Social Backgrounds (323BC-AD70):

Motives behind the Hatred and Racism:

- The Samaritans lived in Samaria, which was sandwiched in the middle of the country between Judea and Galilee *(Acts 1:8)*.
- It's said that there may have been as many Samaritans as Jews in Palestine during the time of Jesus.
- The Samaritans emerged about 400BC as a result of mixed marriages between Jews and Gentiles.
- The Jews regarded them as half-breed bastards.
- The Samaritans constructed their own temple on Mount Gerizim north of Jerusalem. They had their

own version of the first five books of the bible, the books of Moses, *(Pentateuch)*.

- They even claimed that their temple was the true place of worship and insisted that their priests had pure blood ties back to the royal priestly line in the Old Testament.

- To the Jewish mind, Samaritans were worse than pagans because they at least knew better.

- Jeremiah says that Samaritans were at the bottom of the ladder of social stratification. They were hated and despised by Jews *(Jeremiah 23:13)*.

- The scriptures attest to the belligerent racism between the two groups.

- John 4:9 says the *"Jews have no dealings with Samaritans."*

- When Samaritans refuse to give Jesus lodging, James and John are so angry that they beg Jesus to destroy the village with fire *(Luke 9:51-56)*.

- Jewish leaders call Jesus a *"Samaritan"* as a derogatory nickname.

- When Jesus was about twelve years old some Samaritans sneaked into the Jerusalem temple at night and scattered human bones over the temple porch and sanctuary. This outrageous act escalated the Jewish/Samaritan hatred.

- Jews would not eat unleavened bread made by a Samaritan or an animal killed by a Samaritan.

- Intermarriage was absolutely prohibited.

- One Rabbi said, *"He who eats bread of a Samaritan is like one that eats the flesh of swine."*

- Samaritan women were considered perpetual menstruates from the cradle and their husbands perpetually unclean.

- Any place where a Samaritan laid was considered unclean, as was any food or drink, which touched the place.

- A whole village was declared unclean if a Samaritan woman stayed there.[4]

Jesus walked in Focused Obedience

Jesus kept referring to the Father, this is important for us to remember as:

We look away from the natural realm and fasten our gaze onto Jesus *who birthed faith within us and who leads us forward into faith's perfection. His example is this:* **Because his heart was focused on the joy of knowing that you would be his, he endured** *the agony of the cross and conquered its humiliation, and now sits exalted at the right hand of the throne of God!*

(Hebrews 12:2)

We also must keep our eyes fastened on the Lord and remember God has promised that He will speak through us, as He did Jesus.

Jesus walked in obedience, out of His love for the Father, speaking only the words of the Father, and moving in the authority inherited as God's one and only Son whom He dearly loved. We have this same authority because of our inheritance through Christ.

Jesus said,

> My teaching is not my own. It comes from Him who sent me.
>
> *(John 7:16)*

> I do nothing on my own authority but speak just as the Father taught me.
>
> *(John 8:28)*

> For I did not speak of my own accord, but the Father who sent me commanded me what to say and how to say it.
>
> *(John 12:49)*

For example, Smith Wigglesworth had to *hear* the voice of God before He could *speak* the voice of God – *(especially waiting for the right person to come along while on his park bench!)*

> I have given you authority to trample on snakes and scorpions [emblems of demonic power] and **to overcome all the power of the enemy.**
>
> *(Luke 10:19)*

Sent out with a Purpose

When Jesus sent out His disciples He said,

> As you go, preach this message: "Heaven's kingdom realm is accessible, close enough to touch." You must continually bring healing to lepers and to those who are sick, and

make it your habit to break off the demonic presence from people, and raise the dead back to life. **Freely you have received the power of the kingdom, so freely release it to others.**

(Matthew 10:7-8 TPT)

Jesus said that the Kingdom was to be their message. He had healed the sick, so they were to do the same. He had cast out demons, so they were to do the same. Jesus raised the dead, so they were to do that also, using the authority of His name.

Jesus said also in Matthew 10:16 (TPT), *"Now, remember, it is I who sends you out, even though you feel vulnerable as lambs going into a pack of wolves. So be as shrewd as snakes yet as harmless [innocent] as doves."*

He also said when the going got tough not to worry about what to say:

Don't be naive. Some people will impugn your motives, others will smear your reputation — just because you believe in me. Don't be upset when they haul you before the civil authorities.

Without knowing it, they've done you — and me — a favor, given you a platform for preaching the kingdom news! **And don't worry about what you'll say or how you'll say it. The right words will be there; the Spirit of your Father will supply the words.**

(Matthew 10:19-20 MSG)

God desires to work through His people, and when we allow ourselves to be yielded to Him, it is then that we will be able to do the things He does:

> *I tell you the truth, anyone who has faith in me will do what I have been doing. He will do even greater things than these, because I am going to the Father. And I will do whatever you ask in my name, so that the Son may bring glory to the Father. You may ask me for anything in my name, and I will do it.*
>
> *(John 14:12-14)*

When Jesus returned to the Father, He prayed for the Holy Spirit to be given, it is only by His Spirit working in us and through us, that we can move in authority and see the miraculous.

We so often forget it was God who called us into the ministry and prepared works for us to do *(Ephesians 2:10)*. It is His faithfulness to us His sons. As we then hear His voice and move out in obedience, we will not only be faithful but take on a ministry that is also prophetic and fruitful.

It was not only to the twelve that Jesus gave this command. He also sent out seventy-two. When He gave the Great Commission to the church, after He had risen from the dead, He said:

> *All authority in heaven and on earth has been given to me. Therefore go and make disciples of all nations, baptising them in the name of the Father and of the Son and of*

the Holy Spirit. And teaching them everything I have commanded you.

(Matthew 28:18-20)

That same power and authority that the early Christians moved in, is the same power that is available to us today.

❖

CHAPTER 6

Kingdom Authority

His Diplomatic Agents

Paul tells us that we are ambassadors, *"We are therefore Christ's ambassadors as though God were making His appeal through us" (2 Corinthians 5:20).*

We are ambassadors of the Anointed One who carry the message of Christ to the world, as though God were tenderly pleading with them directly through our lips. So we tenderly plead with you on Christ's behalf, "Turn back to God and be reconciled to him."

(2 Corinthians 5:20 TPT)

According to the Passion Translations footnotes: "To be ambassadors for Christ means that we are His diplomatic agents of the highest rank sent to represent King Jesus and authorized to speak on His behalf. **We are the voice of**

heaven to the earth, invested with royal power through the name of Jesus and authority of his blood."

An American Ambassador or Diplomat coming to London, England, and who becomes a resident at the American Embassy, will still in theory be in America. That bit of ground right in the middle of London where the Embassy has been built or established belongs to America! It's out of bounds to the laws of Great Britain.

Diplomatic Immunity

The Ambassador can walk through London and every place where he puts his feet becomes America. We have heard of stories from the press and television where diplomats have enjoyed diplomatic immunity from all sorts of crimes, *(which if you or I had committed them would be in jail!)*

A diplomat then, is seen as representing the interests, and authorities of another country or kingdom.

Likewise, Christians represent the Kingdom of God on earth and although we are here in this world, we are not of it *(John 17:14-16; John 15:19; 2 Corinthians 10:3)*. I am not saying we should have *diplomatic immunity* to break laws *(no!)* As ambassadors though, we aught to be advancing the interests of God's Kingdom:

> *Our struggle is not against flesh and blood, but against the rulers, against the authorities, against the powers of this dark world and against the spiritual forces of evil in the heavenly realms.*
>
> *(Ephesians 6:12)*

We should be pushing these spiritual forces back. *(Making the weight of our legal representation felt in the atmosphere)*. What did God say to Joshua? Every place where you put your foot, I will give to you *(Joshua 1:3)*.

When Seeking Refuge

The following definitions are from the Merriam Webster Dictionary:

Diplomatic Immunity - an international law that gives *foreign diplomats* special rights in the country where they are working. NOTE: Under *diplomatic immunity*, diplomats cannot be arrested and do not have to pay taxes while working in other countries.

Refugee - one that flees especially a person who flees to a foreign country or power to escape danger or persecution.

Asylum - protection from arrest and extradition given especially to **political refugees** by a nation or by an embassy or other agency enjoying freedom from what is required by law for most people.[1]

In 2012 Julian Assange, Australian editor, publisher and activist *(founder of the infamous WikiLeaks)*, sought political refuge in the Ecuadorian Embassy in London.

It has been suggested that disguised as a courier, Julian Assange walked into the Ecuadorian Embassy and was granted asylum by the government of Ecuador, for almost seven years. Such events surrounding the life and political activities of Mr Julian Assange are rather complicated and well documented!

According to one source we read:

"After the 2010 leaks, the United States government launched a criminal investigation into WikiLeaks. In November 2010, Sweden issued an international arrest warrant for Assange, after questioning him months earlier about allegations of sexual assault. Assange denied the allegations, and said they were just a pretext for him to be extradited from Sweden to the United States because of his role in publishing secret American documents.

Assange surrendered to UK police on 7 December 2010 but was released on bail within ten days. Having been unsuccessful in his challenge to the extradition proceedings, he breached his £340,000 bail **in June 2012 to seek asylum from Ecuador.**

In August 2012, Assange was **granted asylum** by Ecuador due to fears of political persecution and possible extradition to the United States. In January 2018, he was **granted Ecuadorian citizenship;** however it was suspended in April 2019. Assange remained in the Embassy of Ecuador in London for almost seven years."[2]

In addition to this, Robert Cryer, Professor of International and Criminal Law of Birmingham Law School posted this article about Assange on the 24 August 2012:

"Still, **Ecuador considers Assange to have a well-founded fear of political persecution, and has granted him diplomatic asylum.** In spite of the frequent use of the term **"diplomatic asylum,"** such a concept is not legally different from **asylum** more generally.

It simply refers to someone who, **rather than travelling to the country in which asylum is sought to seek that status, goes into the embassy of that State in another country to make the claim.**

If that claim is successful, it is important to note, though, that **does not give the applicant diplomatic status. This is crucial; what it means is that although he has been granted asylum, Assange is not immune from UK jurisdiction. Hence, he remains arrestable.**

That does not mean that he can be arrested right away, as **although he is not immune from UK jurisdiction, the Ecuadorean embassy, and its property are."**[3]

He said of Mr Assange, *"... although he has been granted asylum, Assange is not immune;"* meaning that he was susceptible to arrest, the moment he left the building!

This is so important to understand. Much like an umbrella, without one we get wet and without covering of authority, we are very vulnerable indeed, exposed to all the elements trying to bring us down.

Why get wet when you can stay dry? And why be without a protection, when the government of heaven and its legal authority can protect us with impenetrable force.

Though important, we possess much higher rights and privileges in Christ, than just mere political human rights.

So whether we use words like *immunity* or *asylum* when representing our national or personal interests, both represent grace *(the right to legal defence and protection)* but not without authority.

Assange wanted his human rights protected but lacked any authority of his own. The only way he could enjoy refuge under Ecuador for so long was that he came under their legal covering *(immunity and authority).*

In Christ we enjoy an impenetrable immunity because He has given His legal authority to us and not to bricks and mortar! As diplomats from heaven, we represent heaven's interests, not our own.

We also get to enjoy private refuge, because as we represent His interests, He represents ours. God is shelter and refuge, our covering and protection: *"The name of the Lord is a strong tower; the righteous run to it and are safe" (Proverbs 18:10 NKJV);* **"God is our refuge and strength,** *a very present help in trouble. Therefore we will not fear..." (Psalm 46:1-2 NKJV)*

We cannot operate outside true governmental authority and claim to have independent rights! It doesn't work that way. You are subject to and protected by the government in the land you come from. Once you make your allegiance with heaven, you'll realise there's no higher governmental authority than Christ's:

> *Of the greatness of his government and peace there* **will be no end.** *He will reign on David's throne and over his kingdom, establishing and upholding it with justice and righteousness from that time on and forever. The zeal of the Lord Almighty will accomplish this.*
>
> *(Isaiah 9:7)*

*Great and vast is his **dominion.** He will bring immeasurable peace and prosperity.*[4]

(Isaiah 9:7 TPT)

What is an Ambassador?

- He is a Diplomatic Minister of the highest order
- He does not speak in his own name
- What he communicates is not his own opinions or demands, but simply what he has been told or commanded to say
- He does not act on his own authority
- In our case we act on the authority of Christ

How do we have Authority as Ambassadors?

By having the authority of Jesus! For Him it came from His relationship with the Father; now it's the same for us.

For he chose us in him before the creation of the world to be holy and blameless in his sight. In love he predestined us to be adopted as his sons through Jesus Christ, in accordance with his pleasure and will.

(Ephesians 1:4-5)

*Turning to his servants, the father said, "Quick, bring me the best robe, my very own robe, and I will place it on his shoulders. Bring the ring, **the seal of sonship,** and I will put it on his finger. And bring out the best shoes you can find for my son..."*

(Luke 15:22 TPT)

I have added this account of the prodigal son, particularly because of the footnotes here, concerning the transference of authority to the son: *"Culturally, this ring was an emblem of authority, giving the son authority to transact business in the father's name. This was a picture of the seal of the Holy Spirit (Ephesians 1:14). Or 'bring sandals for his feet.' Slaves were barefoot."*

Let me just interject here; there was no mention of washing! *(We know that Jesus washes us with the water of His Word for example Ephesians 5:26 and 1 John 1:9).* But did this prodigal son really still stink like swine when his father draped his own robe around him? Where his feet still unwashed *(like slave's feet),* when he clothed them with, "the best shoes," his servants could find? *(Luke 15:22)*

While it all appears to take place in one film shot or movie scene, it matters little, because it creates this incredible scene of lavished *(heaped, smothered, showered)* love and most of all the extreme redemptive nature of God. This is the divine nature of our heavenly Father - towards us. He exchanges our filthy rags for His own robes of righteousness!

We are all as an unclean thing, and all our righteousnesses are as filthy rags...
(Isaiah 64:6 KJV)

*I will greatly rejoice in the Lord, my soul shall be joyful in my God; for **he hath clothed me with the garments of salvation, he hath covered me with the robe of righteousness.***
(Isaiah 61:10 KJV)

We have been given Matchless Authority

It's this relationship with the Father that's been made possible through Jesus Christ. It's the name of *JESUS* that carries all authority. Even though this authority has been given to us, I still don't cast out demons by the name of Alan Pateman.

No! Only ever in Christ's name; the name given to the church - with the legal right to use it – and by using it we represent Him and act in His stead.

If I am praying for someone, it is as though Jesus Himself was ministering to that person. We are taking Christ's place and acting as Christ's representatives, not only collectively but also individually. **As we use His name - we are using His authority - to carry out His will on the earth.**

We see in the simplicity of Peter's prayer that he knew that he was acting in Jesus' stead, with the same authority that Jesus had. All he had to say to a crippled beggar was, *"In the name of Jesus, rise up and walk" (Acts 3:6).*

Here was Peter the apostle who was in many ways just like you and me. He too had problems with his human nature; he always seemed to be in trouble due to his eagerness. But after Pentecost, Peter totally knew who he was! He had no identity problem, once he knew the true identity of Jesus.

On the day of Pentecost *(Acts 2:1-4)* when the Holy Spirit came upon him, filling and baptizing him with power, gave him incredible boldness and made him stand up with formidable authority, like a lion *(Isaiah 5:26-30).*

Very often when we minister to people, we want to sit them down, make them comfortable and then share all sorts of things with them. What we're really saying to them is this: "I'm in a place of unbelief myself, so what I'm really doing, is trying to get into a place of faith myself!"

Then when we finally get-over-ourselves and finally pray; rarely does anything happen! Which is all an exercise in futility and only manages to bolster collective disbelief.

We have Authority that's not Anaemic

Except Peter knew who he was, straight away he said *"Rise up in the name of Jesus" (Acts 3:6)*. The lame man was obviously reaching out from within his spirit, and Peter could see his faith therefore, *"Taking him by the right hand, he helped him up, and instantly the man's feet and ankles became strong" (Acts 3:7)*.

Jesus said,

> *I will do whatever you ask in my name, so that the son may bring glory to the Father.*
> *(John 14:13)*

> *Go to all the world and preach the good news to all creation.*
> *(Mark 16:15)*

Notice no words of ambiguity are used in the next passage of scripture, such anaemic words as, *might* or *possibly* but always in the affirmative like, *"... they will recover"* and stated with great certainty, as matter of fact and not in fragile suggestive terms:

*He said to them, "Go into all the world and preach the gospel to every creature. He who believes and is baptized __will__ be saved; but he who does not believe will be condemned. And these **signs __will__ follow** those who believe: In My name they __will__ cast out demons; they __will__ speak with new tongues; they __will__ take up serpents; and if they drink anything deadly, it __will by no means__ hurt them; they __will__ lay hands on the sick, and they __will__ recover."*

(Mark 16:15-18 NKJV)

The legal right to use the name JESUS CHRIST is all ours! So let's boldly declare:

WE HAVE AUTHORITY

❖

CHAPTER 7

Powerful Armour
for Spiritual Warfare

Dressed for Victory

Now my beloved ones, I have saved these most important truths for last: Be supernaturally infused with strength through your life-union with the Lord Jesus. **Stand victorious with the force of his explosive power flowing in and through you.**

*Put on God's complete set of armor provided for us, so that you will **be protected as you fight against the evil strategies of the accuser!***

Your hand-to-hand combat is not with human beings, but with the highest principalities and authorities operating

97

in rebellion under the heavenly realms. For they are a powerful class of demon-gods* and evil spirits that hold this dark world in bondage.

Because of this, **you must wear all the armor that God provides so you're protected as you confront the slanderer,** *for you are destined for all things and* **will rise victorious.**

Put on truth as a belt to strengthen you to stand in triumph. **Put on holiness as the protective armor that covers your heart.** *Stand on your feet alert, then you'll always be ready to share the blessings of peace.*

In every battle, take faith as your wrap-around shield, for it is able to extinguish the blazing arrows coming at you from the Evil One! Embrace the power of salvation's full deliverance, like a helmet to protect your thoughts from lies. And **take the mighty razor-sharp Spirit-sword of the spoken Word of God.**

Pray passionately in the Spirit, as you constantly intercede with every form of prayer at all times. Pray the blessings of God upon all his believers.

(Ephesians 6:10-18 TPT)

According to the footnotes the classical Greek word used in verse 13 [*demon-gods*] is often used to refer to conjuring up pagan deities — supreme powers of darkness mentioned in occult rituals.

On the Winning Side

While in this world we are in the middle of the conflict between the kingdom of God and the kingdom of darkness, but praise God we as Christians are now on the winning side, because Jesus has already declared victory on our behalf.

Then I heard a loud voice in heaven say: "Now have come the salvation and the power and the kingdom of our God, and the authority of His Christ.

For the accuser of our brothers, who accuses them before our God day and night, has been hurled down. *They overcame him by the blood of the Lamb and by the **word of their testimony;** they did not love their lives so much as to shrink from death."*

(Revelation 12:10-11)

Satan and his hosts are already defeated but we need to understand that every Christian needs to be trained in the pulling down of strongholds. The armed forces would think it foolish to send out troops that have not been trained and equipped for battle. Every soldier has to go through rigorous combat training **to learn the correct rules of engagement.**

*For though we walk in the world, we do not fight according to **this world's rules of warfare.***

(2 Corinthians 10:3 VOICE)

Knowing our Spiritual Weapons

They are fully trained and equipped for the battle in all areas of attack and defence. This is easy to understand, when looking at the reality of war through television and seeing the devastation that war inflicts.

If only we could see the same devastation in the spirit realm, Satan and his armies of demonic powers strategically and even tactically planning invasions upon mankind. We then would see the reality of war.

> *The weapons we fight with are not the weapons of the world. On the contrary, they have divine power to* **demolish strongholds.**
> *(2 Corinthians 10:4)*

> *Does not My word burn like fire? Does it not shatter rock like a* **strong hammer?**
> *(Jeremiah 23:29 VOICE)*

> *From that time on, preaching was part of Jesus' work. "Repent, for the kingdom of heaven is at hand."*
> *(Matthew 4:17 VOICE)*

Weapons that Demolish Strongholds:

- The name of Jesus and authority *(Mark 16:16)*
- The Spirit *(Matthew 12:28)*
- The Word, it is written *(hammer - Jeremiah 23:29) (Matthew 4:17)*
- The blood *(Revelation 12:11)*
- The testimony *(Revelation 12:11)*
- The gifts of the Spirit *(1 Corinthians 12:1-11)*
- The power of God, "THE ANOINTING" *(Acts 10:38)*

- Anointed music

- Praise

- Fasting *(Mark 9:29)*

- Repentance

- Groaning, weeping and travailing prayer

- Fight the good fight of faith *(1 Timothy 1:18)*

- The armour of God *(Ephesians 6:10)*

- Angels *(Psalm 34:7)*

- Submission *(James 4:7)*

- Humbling ourselves *(Proverbs 16:18)*

Revealed in Ephesians 6:13-18:

*Therefore put on the **full armour** of God, so that when the day of evil comes, you may be able to stand your ground, and after you have done everything, to stand.*

*Stand firm then, with the **belt of truth** buckled round your waist, with the **breastplate of righteousness** in place, and with your **feet fitted with the readiness** that comes from the gospel of peace. In addition to all this, take up the **shield of faith,** with which you can extinguish all the flaming arrows of the evil one. Take the **helmet of salvation** and the **sword of the Spirit,** which is the **word of God.***

*And **pray in the Spirit** on all occasions with all kinds of prayers and requests. With this in mind, be alert and always keep on praying for all the saints.*

Truth, our Safety Belt

God's truth enables us to move into battle. For a Roman soldier the belt was used to tuck up his tunic, it was the first piece of armour he would put on. It ensured that he could fight unhindered by a flowing garment. *"Tuck up your tunic"* or *"Gird up your loins,"* means to prepare for activity as seen in Exodus 12:11, be dressed in readiness *(Luke 12:35)*. Prepare your minds for action *(1 Peter 1:13)*.

Paul states that for Christians our belt needs to be God's truth *(Ephesians 6:14)*, with it we can move freely and quickly. Putting on God's truth then means living out God's Word - being honest, sincere in our faith and not full of religious hypocrisy. So the **belt of truth** refers to the Christian's character and integrity, a life-style that conforms to the Word of God.

In order to live out a **life-style** for God, means that we have to know God's Word and what it says about the Christian way of life. We have to be prepared to live and act upon His Word; it is an act of will *(1 John 5:2)*. Character is very important, **character not brute force is the first step in winning battles against Satan.**

Righteousness A Breastplate

The breastplate covered the front of the soldier; it was a major piece of equipment that protected the soldier's heart.

*So may the words of my mouth, my meditation-thoughts, and **every movement of my heart** be always pure and* *pleasing, acceptable before your eyes, my only Redeemer, my Protector-God.*

(Psalm 19:14 TPT)

Then, as you unwrap my words, they will impart true life and radiant health into the very core of your being.

*So **above all, guard the affections of your heart,** for they affect all that you are. **Pay attention to the welfare of your innermost being,** for from there flows the wellspring of life.*

(Proverbs 4:22-23 TPT)

According to the footnotes the Hebrew word used for heart in verse 23, includes our: *thoughts, will, discernment, and affections.*

Clearly we must be careful to guard our innermost beings. The enemy will fire arrows in the form of criticism, accusations, condemnation, spiritual pride and a host of other things *(Ephesians 6:16)*. When our hearts are under the covering of God's righteousness we are fully protected, therefore we should stand in God's righteousness.

Righteousness from God comes through faith in Jesus Christ to all who believe, *(Romans 3:22)*; our own righteousness God considers as filthy rags.

His righteousness comes through the redemption work of the blood. It is the Lord's righteousness with which we are covered; this is our inheritance as sons who have been adopted through Jesus Christ, through the redemption and forgiveness of our sins *(Ephesians 1:5-7)*.

In Ephesians 4:24 and 5:9 Paul uses righteousness to refer to being upright in character and conduct.

> *You were taught, with regard to your former way of life, to put off your old self, which is being corrupted by its deceitful desires [delusions]; to be **made new in the attitudes of your minds;** and to put on the **new self,** created to be like God in true righteousness and holiness.*
> *(Ephesians 4:22-24)*

> *We do not have the excuse of ignorance, everything – and I do mean everything – connected with that old way of life has to go. It's rotten through and through. Get rid of it! **And then take on an entirely new way of life – a God-fashioned life,** a life renewed from the inside and working itself into your conduct **as God accurately reproduces his character in you.***
> *(Ephesians 4:24 MSG)*

> *God has re-created you all over again in his perfect righteousness, and you now belong to him in the realm of true holiness.*
> *(Ephesians 4:24b TPT)*

We must be willing to change from our old ways and **put on the new self** and turn to that which the Word of God states for our lives. Righteousness then is a heart condition! A heart that is determined for the right course of life.

Peace, Prepared to Share

A Roman soldier wore protective and supportive footwear; this footwear would be tied to the ankles and shins with ornamental straps. They were boots equipping them for long marches and for giving them a solid footing.

Shoes *(Ephesians 6:15)* indicate that we always need to be prepared to share the gospel of peace at all times, this means we must know how to tell unbelievers about Christ, being open to the Holy Spirit's leading in specific situations.

The Great Commission

*Jesus came to them and said, all authority in heaven and on earth has been given to me. Therefore go and make disciples of all nations, baptizing them in the name of the Father and of the Son and of the Holy Spirit, and teaching them to **obey everything** I have commanded you. And surely I am with you always, to the very end of the age.*
(Matthew 28:18-20)

Jesus has commissioned all true disciples to preach the gospel. We have been sent as Christ's ambassadors to preach *reconciliation to all the world* (2 Corinthians 5:20).

God has promised that we will be witnesses in the power of the Holy Spirit *(Acts 12:8)*. Remember our commission is to make disciples not converts. **True disciples change lives not just their minds!**

As we share the gospel of peace, I must say only when done in love. Then the shoes like the rest of our armour are to enable us to stand. What soldier would want to be caught by the enemy with his boots off? Our shoes like the rest of our armour should always be on! This piece of equipment enables a soldier to hold his ground, to the defence and confirmation of the gospel.

Writing to persecuted Christians, Peter says:

> **Be ready at all times** *to answer anyone who asks you to explain the hope you have in you.*
>
> > *(1 Peter 3:15)*

> *...yet [do it] with gentleness and respect.*
>
> > *(1 Peter 3:15 AMP)*

> *...and always with the utmost courtesy.*
>
> > *(1 Peter 3:15 MSG)*

In other words be ready always with your boots on.

In Acts of the Apostles it teaches us to preach the gospel, not to argue or to push it down people's throats but to testify to what He *(Christ)* has done for us. Remember the old saying, *"Practice what you preach,"* people must see an outward sign; our lives must be a testimony to the love and power of God.

It is not only what we say that matters; it is also what people *see.* **Because, although words can be very powerful they can also be very cheap indeed!**

❖

CHAPTER 8

Faith is our Shield

Extinguishing and Resisting

A Roman soldier usually carried two shields but the one I will refer to here is the larger of the two. It normally measured four and a half feet high by two and a half feet wide and was oval shaped. It consisted of two layers of wood glued together and covered with leather; the soldier would squat behind it.

Saturated yet not Burdensome

Flaming arrows would be dipped in pitch, lit, and fired at the Roman soldier but frequently before battles, the soldiers would dip their shields in water *(heavy!)* to extinguish the flaming arrows, which would bury themselves into their shields. These shields would cover the soldiers from head to foot, extinguishing the arrows and resisting the enemy.

Now, we could assume hypothetically that a water-saturated leather and wood shield like this would totally weigh us down.

On the contrary we know that scripture says, *"We are washed with the water of the Word"* (Ephesians 5:26) and that *"...his commands don't weigh us down as heavy burdens"* (1 John 5:3 TPT). Including that His, *"yoke is easy and... burden is light!"* (Matthew 11:30) So it all depends on the water you saturate it with!

Ultimately this shield of faith has the capacity to completely protect us and quench the enemy's onslaught without exhausting, **only invigorating us in the process.**

Resisting Isolation and Depression

*Your enemy the devil prowls around like a roaring lion looking for someone to devour. **Resist him, standing firm in the faith.***

(1 Peter 5:8-9)

*Be well balanced and always alert, because your enemy, the devil, roams around incessantly, like a roaring lion looking for its prey to devour. **Take a decisive stand against him and resist his every attack with strong, vigorous faith.***

(1 Peter 5:9 TPT)

The footnote here says, *"The implication in the context is that if you do not bring your worries and cares to God, **the devil will use depression and discouragement to devour you.** Just as lions go after the feeble, the young, and the stragglers, so the* *enemy of our souls will always seek out those who are **isolated,** **alone, or depressed to devour them."***

Faith Always Shows in Action

Clearly we need to fix our eyes on Jesus, the author and perfecter of our faith, *(Hebrews 12:2)*. When we take our commission seriously and go on the offensive in challenging Satan, he fights back with flaming arrows. He attacks us and everything associated with us: our church, marriage partner, children, business - everything. **Our only shield against these attacks is FAITH.**

We need to believe in God's ability to protect us and have confidence in His Word, for **faith always shows in action.** James 2:17 says, *"Faith by itself, if not accompanied by action is dead."* Faith on its own is dead, we may have faith but **if we are not acting in faith and on faith, then it amounts to nothing.**

If Faith isn't Now – it's Not Faith

Now faith *is being sure of what we hope for and **certain** of what we do not see.*

(Hebrews 11:1)

*...**fully persuaded** that God had power to do what he had promised.*

(Romans 4:21)

Faith that is the substance of things hoped for is always now faith. **If faith is not now, it is not faith.** If it is not faith that is present tense, it is not the substance of things hoped for. Hope is always out there in the future.

It is easy to miss the application of faith; very often we confess hope, *"Well, I believe God is going to do this sometime."* But God has done all He is ever going to do about our healing, finance, our foe etc.

God has already spoken and made promises to His children about their circumstances, for God's will is revealed in His Word. **His Word *is* His Will.** Faith is an active moving force, which moves Christians forward.

Jesus said to His disciples that if they had faith in God and did not doubt in their hearts, whatever they said would come to pass, this Word is the same Word for us.

> *Jesus replied,* **"Let the faith of God be in you!** *Listen to the truth I speak to you: If someone says to this mountain with great faith and having no doubt, 'Mountain, be lifted up and thrown into the midst of the sea,' and believes that what he says will happen it will be done. This is the reason* **I urge you to boldly believe** *for whatever you ask for in prayer — believe that you have received it and it will be yours."*
>
> (Mark 11:22-24 TPT)

The footnote says: *"The mountain and the sea can also be metaphors. Mountains in the bible can refer to kingdoms, and the sea represents the nations... This truth Jesus brings us is more than hyperbole; it is the active power of faith to take and carry the power and authority of the mountain — God's kingdom realm — with us wherever we go."*

Salvation's Helmet

This piece of equipment was usually made of a tough bronze or iron alloy. It often had a hinged visor that added protection, nothing short of an axe could penetrate it. Of course, it protected the head, the source of our thought life *(Ephesians 6:17)*.

Many Christians it would seem are incapacitated because they do not seem to know how to protect their thought lives. Satan will bombard our minds with fear, hatred, suspicion, depression, mistrust and a host of other distractions. The bible tells us to renew our minds:

Do not conform any longer to the pattern of this world, but be transformed by the renewing of your mind. Then you will be able to test and approve what God's will is - his good, pleasing and perfect will.

(Romans 12:2)

Stop imitating the ideals and opinions of the culture around you, [don't be squeezed into the mold of this present age], but be inwardly transformed by the Holy Spirit through a total reformation of how you think. This will empower you to discern God's will as you live a beautiful life, satisfying and perfect in his eyes.

(Romans 12:2 TPT)

Embracing what God does for you is the best thing you can do for him. ***Don't become so well-adjusted to your culture that you fit into it without even thinking.*** *Instead, fix your attention on God. You'll be changed from the inside out.*

Readily recognize what he wants from you, and quickly respond to it. **Unlike the culture around you, always dragging you down to its level of immaturity, God brings the best out of you, develops well-formed maturity in you.**

(Romans 12:2 MSG)

Protecting your Most Powerful Asset

As an additional side-note here, my wife and I have been watching a YouTube channel of late, called *Off The Ranch (a.k.a. Demolition Ranch / Bunker branding / Vet Ranch etc.)* and the YouTube personality running these channels is simply called "Matt."

Now Matt is an eclectic, comical and full-throttle type of personality, who goes from naught-to-sixty in seconds. He's a veterinarian, who spends his life, rescuing animals, doing gun reviews; home demolition/renovation etc., and you name it!

However, on one particular episode of *Demolition Ranch,* Matt climbs out of his home gun-safe *(which is the size of a walk-in closet!)* surrounded by countless expensive firearms and ammunition, only to say:

"Do you know what the world's most powerful weapon is?" Pointing to his forehead asserts, *"It's not the atom/ nuclear bomb, IT'S YOUR MIND - SO PROTECT IT!"*

I welcomed this, because today guys like Matt are called *influencers.* They have massive influence on the culture and amass a global following of millions of loyal subscribers and regular viewership.

I have no interest in guns personally; but his simple remarks about not underestimating the *mind* were stirring. We can talk a lot about all the modern mental-health issues plaguing society, but the fact remains; God's Word provides the single best defence/offence when it comes to mind health and protection.

Mental Health and the Spoken Word of God

The one thing that can stop us going insane is the SPOKEN WORD OF GOD, which has the power to cleanse and restore our minds. Consequently it is important that we read and meditate on His Word and keep His commands and remain obedient to them.

We must read, meditate and *speak* the Word continually, taking captive *[filter]* every thought to make it obedient to Christ *(2 Corinthians 10:5)*.

> *Do not let this book of the law depart from your mouth;* **meditate on it day and night,** *so that you may be careful to do everything written in it. Then you will be prosperous and successful.*
>
> *(Joshua 1:8)*

The Vine's Complete Expository Dictionary says that *to meditate* means: *to moan, growl, utter and speak.* This word is common to both ancient and modern Hebrew. Found only 25 times in the Hebrew Old Testament, it seems to be an onomatopoetic term, reflecting the sighing and low sounds one may make while musing, at least as the ancients practiced it.

This meaning is seen in its first occurrence in the text: *"This book of the law shall not depart out of thy mouth; but thou shalt meditate therein day and night…" (Joshua 1:8 KJV)* Perhaps the most famous reference *"to meditating"* on the law day and night is Psalm 1:2.

Hagah also expresses the *"growl"* of lions *(Isaiah 31:4)* and the *"mourning"* of doves *(Isaiah 38:14)*. When the word is used in the sense of *"to mourn,"* it apparently emphasizes the sorrowful sounds of mourning, as seen in this parallelism: *"Therefore will I howl for Moab, and I will cry out for all Moab; mine heart shall mourn for the men of Kir-heres" (Jeremiah 48:31).*

The idea that mental exercise, planning, often is accompanied by low talking seems to be reflected by Proverbs 24:1-2: *"Be not thou envious against evil men, … for their heart studieth destruction, and their lips talk of mischief."*

The Weaknesses of the Natural Mind:

- It is hostile to God *(Romans 8:5-7)*

- Things of God are foolish to the natural mind *(2 Corinthians 4:4)*

- The natural mind is the source of violent and evil desires *(Ephesians 2:3)*

- It is futile in its thinking, darkened in understanding *(Ephesians 4:17-18)*

We have not received the spirit of the world but the ***Spirit who is from God,*** *that we may understand what God has freely given us. This is what we speak, not in words taught us by human wisdom but in words taught by the Spirit,* ***expressing spiritual truths in spiritual words.***

The man without the Spirit does not accept the things that come from the Spirit of God, for they are foolishness to him, and he cannot understand them, because they are spiritually discerned.

(1 Corinthians 2:12-14)

We articulate these realities with the words imparted to us by the Spirit and not with the words taught by human wisdom. ***We join together Spirit-revealed truths with Spirit-revealed words.***

Someone living on an entirely human level rejects the revelations of God's Spirit, for they make no sense to him. ***He can't understand the revelations of the Spirit because they are only discovered by the illumination of the Spirit.***

(1 Corinthians 2:13-14 TPT)

Renewing the Mind

So we need the Holy Spirit before we can understand the things of God. So how do we go about renewing the mind?

Principles:

- We must completely surrender our minds to the Lord *(Romans 12:1)*

- We must submit our thinking to the Cross - Jesus *(Ephesians 4:20)*

- Make a deliberate choice about the place of our minds *(Colossians 3:2)*

- Read and meditate on the cleansing power of God's Word *(Joshua 1:8)*

Action:

- We must examine and test the content of our thought life *(Philippians 4:4-8)*

- Immediately refuse every wrong thought *(Philippians 4:6)*

- Read and meditate on the Word *(Joshua 1:8)*

Signs of a Renewed Mind:

- Spiritual understanding increased *(Ephesians 1:18)*

- A change of life through understanding truth *(Philippians 4:8-9)*

The mind then becomes the vehicle of the Holy Spirit, His gifts, discernment and revelation.

❖

CHAPTER 9

The Word Our Sword

Two Mouthed Sword

This sixth piece of equipment that Paul uses as an example for spiritual protection is for our defence and our offence *(Ephesians 6:17)*. The sword referred to here was small, approximately twelve to fourteen inches long, it was pinpoint sharp and had a blade that could cut in any direction.

In Hebrew 4:12 it says:

For the word of God is living and active. Sharper than any double edged sword, it penetrates even to dividing soul and spirit, joints and marrow; it judges the thoughts and attitudes of the heart. Nothing in all creation is hidden from God's sight. Everything is uncovered and laid bare before the eyes of him to whom we must give account.

The Word of God is both our weapon of defence against sin and of offence against demonic invasion. The apostle Paul uses the **Rhema Word,** which means a word that is spoken, words spoken by the power of the Holy Spirit to assist us in defending ourselves against the enemy. We are also, of course, told to proclaim the very manifold wisdom of God to the rulers and authorities in the heavenly realms *(Ephesians 3:10-12).*

This is exactly what Jesus did when He encountered Satan or his demons. With authority and power He spoke the Word and Satan fled *(each time).*

Double Mouthed with Double Impact

We have the living Word of God, which is full of energy, and it pierces more sharply than a two-edged sword. It will even penetrate to the very core of our being where soul and spirit, bone and marrow meet! It interprets and reveals the true thoughts and secret motives of our hearts.

(Hebrews 4:12 TPT)

Notice that the footnote here suggests that rather than a two-edged sword; instead it could mean a *"... two-mouthed sword." God speaks His word, then we, in agreement, also speak His word and it becomes a two-mouthed-sword.*

This proposes an interesting twist and reminds me of James 1:8, another occasion where a *"double"* is mentioned in scripture, but in the negative sense. The original language again proposes that a double-minded person is actually a *double-souled* or *double-spirited!* Which provides a fascinating reference to someone who possesses divided interests and split loyalties between God and the world - someone who is always vacillating, *(in opinion and purpose)*. Someone stuck in the valley of decision.

ONLY AS WE VOICE GOD'S WORD IN TOTAL AGREEMENT can His sword become double-mouthed with double-impact!

As we speak God's Word *(like a child imitating their father)*, light begins to dispel darkness, bringing freedom and liberty. Satan will bring temptation in many different forms, even trying to deceive us with the Word of God itself. **We must discern if God is actually speaking to us.**

In 1 Corinthians 2:15 it states that, *"the Spiritual man makes judgements about all things."* Jesus of course knew the Word as He was the Word and was able to discern truth, which is the Word of God, rather than to allow His feelings to rule His decisions.

Believe on His Word

We have confidence when we pray the promises of God and say what He says,

> I tell you the truth, if anyone says to this mountain, "Go, throw yourself into the sea," and **does not doubt** in his heart but believes that what he says will happen, it will be done for him. Therefore I tell you, whatever you ask for in prayer, believe that you have received it, and it will be yours.
>
> *(Mark 11:23-24)*

The above scripture is telling us to believe and not doubt, but goes on to say in verse 25:

And when you stand praying, if you hold anything against anyone, forgive him, so that your Father in heaven may forgive you your sins.

We must have no unforgiveness in our hearts but must come before Him with pure hearts *(Psalm 66:18)*, with nothing against anyone.

- Confess our Sin *(1 John 1:9)*
- Forgive as an act of will *(Matthew 6:14)*
- Believe that you have received your forgiveness *(Matthew 6:14)*

Prayer and Intercession are Indispensible

Prayer is a powerful weapon, Ephesians 6:18 says: *"pray with all kinds of prayers"* this includes praying in tongues. There is power in intercession and we know that Jesus is interceding for us *(Romans 8:34).*

*Who then is the one who condemns? No one. Christ Jesus who died – more than that, who was raised to life – **is at the right hand of God and is also interceding for us.***
(Romans 8:34)

*So how could he possibly condemn us **since he is continually praying for our triumph?***
(Romans 8:34 TPT)

The footnote here says: *"Not only does the Holy Spirit pray for us, so does Jesus Christ. **Two divine intercessors are praying for you each day. Two-thirds of the Trinity are actively engaged in intercession for us.** This is typified by the incident of Moses interceding on the mountain for Israel's victory with one hand held high by Aaron (the high priest, a type of Jesus, our High Priest) and Hur (or "light," a metaphor for the Holy Spirit, who prays with divine illumination for our good). See Exodus 17:9-13; Hebrews 7:25; 9:24.*

John Wesley once said, *"It seems that God is limited by our prayer life, that He can do nothing for humanity unless someone asks Him."* Despite this, God is still in complete control. He has chosen prayer and intercession as the instrument for the release of His power on earth through His believers.

His Power at our Disposal

The power of God is at our disposal, waiting for us to call Him into action, so long as we are being obedient and living His Word.

God is looking for men and women who will stand in the gap. Who will intercede, who will spend time in an act of intercession? Often when we talk about the harvest, often we're only interested in being part of the reaping end of the action!

Yet we must be willing to invest as much time standing in the gap. We can only be fruitful if prayer has been the overriding precedent and intercession the practicing standard. Only then can we see fruit in ministry.

In Joel 2:13 we are told to *"Rend your hearts and not your garments"* or as two other translations say: *"Change your life, not just your clothes" (MSG); "Rip the wickedness out of your hearts; don't just tear your clothing" (VOICE).*

We need to give birth, *"Yet no sooner is Zion in labour than she gives birth to her children" (Isaiah 66:8).*

This is a very profound statement, taking Zion to represent the church, if we go into labour through intercession and into a state of birth, praying then becomes an active event.

The Birthing Experience

Every mother will know that at the time of giving birth, it is a very active - not necessarily pleasant - experience! The mother does not necessarily care who hears her or even watches at the time.

She is so taken up with the need to give birth. Intercession *(travailing in the Spirit)* is giving birth to the things of God and can be a noisy affair. Just like groans of travail precede the birth of a child, so too with Holy Spirit inspired intercession.

Travailing in the Spirit brings to birth new life, new hope, and new possibilities for those who are trapped in seemingly impossible situations.

God promises in Joel that when you rend your heart, crying out in birth, *"afterwards, I will pour out my Spirit on all people," (Joel 2:13, 28).*

I know from watching the birth of our own children, that the process is agony as Jesus foretold. But the moment the child is laid upon the mother's breast, the pain is forgotten and the joy of new birth overwhelms her.

When interceding, there will be times when we will recognise in our spirits that the breakthrough has happened. We'll know this breakthrough by the experience of intense joy. We can rejoice that our prayers have been received and answered in the spirit realm. That is when we see results in the natural realm, but not before the breakthrough has been given.

Completely Dependent on His Power

Intercession is a very powerful weapon - in the onslaught of the enemy. If we want to see the Spirit of God move mightily on a housing estate for example, then we must be willing to intercede and get into an attitude of bringing God's will into being, travailing for them. Then we will reap the harvest that God has prepared.

> My dear children, for whom I am again in the pains of childbirth until Christ is formed in you.
>
> (Galatians 4:19)

Paul was constantly in a place of weeping before God for his people. This then should also be the place for us. Prayer not only produces individual power, but it also produces corporate power as well.

We must recognize that we have no power of our own, but as we come before God in obedience, in submission completely surrendered unto him. Dead to self, with a servant's heart, completely broken before Him, then He will release His power into our lives. We must depend on His power, the power of the Holy Spirit and not depend on man-made power.

> *Not by might nor by power, but by my Spirit, says the Lord Almighty.*
>
> (Zechariah 4:6)

> *You can't force these things. They only come about through my Spirit...*
>
> (Zechariah 4:6 MSG)

In ourselves we can do nothing, but in Christ we can do all things, because it is He who gives us the strength by His Holy Spirit so that we can be successful in our prayer lives.

God's Word must be foremost, because as we feed on His Word we are building His Words into our inner lives, *"Build yourselves up... make progress, **rise like an edifice higher and higher,** praying in the Holy Spirit"* (Jude 20 AMPC).

In Prayer we must:

- Pray, Father in the name of Jesus *(John 16:23)*
- Pray, according to His will *(1 John 5:14)*
- Pray, without doubting *(James 1:6-7)*
- Pray, with a pure heart *(Psalm 66:18)*
- Pray, fervently *(Luke 18:7)*
- Thank God, for answered Prayer *(Colossians 4:6)*

We must remember that Jesus has made us more than conquerors *(Romans 8:37)*, and that we have power in prayer because:

- He has set us free *(Colossians 1:13)*
- He was triumphant at the Cross *(Colossians 2:15)*
- We can approach the throne of God with confidence *(Hebrews 4:1)*
- Satan is under our feet *(Luke 10:19)*
- We have authority in Jesus' name *(Matthew 10:1)*
- We have overcome him *(Satan)* by the blood of the Lamb *(Revelation 12:11)*

❖
Endnotes

Acknowledgement

1. Reverend Dr Tunde Bakare (Pastor, Teacher, Lawyer, Author, Activist); https://thecitadelglobal.org; https://en.wikipedia.org/wiki/Tunde_Bakare; http://tundebakare.com; https://lraglobal.org/the-citadel

Preface

1. The Reality of a Warrior, by Dr Alan Pateman, Publisher: APMI Publications, United Kingdom, Printed by Merseyside Printing Company, United Kingdom, 1991

Introduction

1. Army of the Dawn, by Rick Joyner, Publisher: Morning Star Publications Inc., Fort Mill, South Carolina, USA, 2015, p103

Chapter 1 The Name of Jesus

1. TPT Footnotes: Between verse 21 and verse 22 the glorious resurrection of Jesus takes place. The music is elevated to a higher key as victory is sounded forth. "My people gather" is a reference to the church that was birthed through his resurrection glory. (See also v25)

2. TPT Footnotes: "Twelve legions." A legion was a detachment of **six thousand** Roman soldiers. Jesus could have called down **seventy-two thousand angels** to come to his aid. The number twelve was a

reminder to the twelve disciples that God had more than enough protection for them all. Note: the Amplified bible claims 80,000!

Chapter 3 Authority to use His Name

1. Ever Increasing Faith, by Smith Wigglesworth, Publisher: Pyramid Publications for the Gospel Publishing House, 1973

Chapter 4 The Meaning of the Word Authority

1. Vine's Expository Dictionary of New Testament Words, by W.E. VINE, Printed by Lowe & Brydone Printers Ltd, Thetford, Norfolk

2. Charles Haddon Spurgeon, CSB Spurgeon Study Bible, by Holman Bible Publishers, Nashville, Tennessee, USA. All Rights Reserved. Christian Standard Bible®. Copyright ©2017 by Holman Bible Publishers. Christian Standard Bible® and CSB® are federally registered trademarks of Holman Bible Publishers

3. The Complete Works of E.M. Bounds, Publisher: Start Publishing LLC. All rights reserved, including the right to reproduce this book or portions thereof in any form whatsoever. First Start Publishing eBook edition October 2012. Start Publishing is a registered trademark of Start Publishing LLC. Manufactured in the United States of America, p66 e-copy

4. The Complete Works of E.M. Bounds, p67 and 68 e-copy

Chapter 5 Authority for Warfare

1. TPT Footnote of Verse 3: Aramaic "rebellious castles" - demonic strongholds/centres of opposition

2. TPT Footnote of Verse 5: Faulty patterns of thought that defy God's authority

3. http://www.oxfordbiblicalstudies.com/article/opr/t94/e1667

4. Excerpts taken from LICU Course Syllabus, THE-214 Understanding the Political, Religious & Social Backgrounds (323BC-AD70), by Dr Alan Pateman, Publisher: APMI Publications, Lucca, Italy, 2007, p16-17

Chapter 6 Kingdom Authority

1. https://www.merriam-webster.com/dictionary/asylum, the date accessed was January 23rd 2020

2. https://en.wikipedia.org/wiki/Julian_Assange, the date accessed was January 23rd 2020

3. https://www.birmingham.ac.uk/news/thebirminghambrief/items/2012/08/Julian-Assange-Asylum-and-Immunity-An-Arresting-Issue.aspx

4. TPT Footnotes: *"His authority will continually expand."* The Hebrew word *misrah,* found only here in vv. 6 and 7, can be translated *"empire, governmental authority, dominion."*

Bible translations

- Unless otherwise indicated, all scriptural quotations are from the HOLY BIBLE, NEW INTERNATIONAL VERSION ®. NIV ®. Copyright © 1973, 1978, 1984 by the International Bible Society. Used by permission of Zondervan Publishing House. All rights reserved.

- Scripture quotations marked AMP are taken from the Amplified® Bible, Copyright © 2015 by The Lockman Foundation. Used by permission. (www.Lockman.org)

- Scripture references marked AMPC are taken from the Amplified® Bible (AMPC), Copyright © 1954, 1958, 1962, 1964, 1965, 1987 by The Lockman Foundation. Used by permission. www.Lockman.org

- Scripture references marked KJV are taken from the King James Version of the bible.

- Scripture quotations marked MSG are taken from The Message. Copyright © 1993, 1994, 1995, 1996, 2000, 2001, 2002. Used by permission of NavPress Publishing Group.

- Scripture quotations marked NKJV are taken from the New King James Version®. Copyright © 1982 by Thomas Nelson, Inc. Used by permission. All rights reserved.

- Scripture quotations marked TLB are taken from The Living Bible. Copyright © 1971 by Tyndale House Foundation. Used by permission of Tyndale House Publishers Inc., Carol Stream, Illinois 60188. All rights reserved.

- Scripture quotations marked TPT are from The Passion Translation®. Copyright © 2017, 2018 by Passion & Fire Ministries, Inc. Used by permission. All rights reserved. ThePassionTranslation.com

❖

Ministry Profile

Doctor Alan Pateman, an apostle, is the President and Founder of **"Alan Pateman Ministries International"** (APMI), which was established in England back in 1987, a Christian-based *(parachurch)* non-profit and non-denominational outreach. This ministry is now focusing in two main areas: First **"Connecting for Excellence"** Apostolic Networking (CFE) and secondly, the teaching arm, **"LifeStyle International Christian University"** (LICU).

CFE is a multi-facetted missions organisation with the purpose of connecting leaders for divine opportunities and building lasting relationships, to touch the lives of leaders literally the world over. Apostle Dr Alan Pateman has to date ordained more than 500 ministers in over 50 NATIONS. In addition there are ministries, churches and schools who are in Association or Affiliation, looking to him for apostolic counsel and oversight.

Secondly LICU, which was founded in 2007, is a study program to help people discover their purpose and destiny. A global network of university campuses and correspondence students, demonstrating the Supernatural Kingdom of God through Doctrinal, Apostolic and Prophetic Teaching. Dr Alan holds the position of President/CEO, Professor of Theology, Biblical Studies and Apostolic Ministry. LICU is exploding throughout Europe, Asia and Africa, enhancing the Body of Christ

Dr Alan has authored more than 35 books including numerous teaching materials and LICU university courses (30) along with hundreds of Truth for the Journey articles on kingdom lifestyle *(that are regularly distributed globally via the internet).*

He is recognised as an Apostle, Bishop, Leadership Mentor, University Educator, Motivational Speaker, Connector and Author, who has also been featured on national and international TV and radio networks throughout the years.

Currently Apostle Alan, his wife Dr Jennifer reside in Lucca *(Tuscany)* Italy and travel out from their Apostolic Company.

- Alan Pateman Ph.D., D.Min., D.D., M.A., B.Th.

Academic Background

Dr. Alan Pateman attended several colleges throughout his training *(including studying Theology at Roffey Place, Horsham, UK and a Member of Kerygma - with Rev. Colin Urquhart and Dr. Bob Gordon - 1985-1987)* before being awarded a Doctorate of Divinity *(2006)* in recognition of his lifetime achievements by the International College of Excellence, now "DanEl Christian College" *(President: Dr. Robb Thompson USA)* also "Life Christian University" *(Dr. Douglas Wingate USA)* where he also earned a Bachelor of Theology B.Th. *(2006),* a Master of Arts in Theology M.A., a Doctor of Ministry in Theology D.Min., *(2007)* and Doctor of Philosophy in Theology Ph.D. *(2013)* from LICU.

❖

To Contact the Author

Please email:

Alan Pateman Ministries International

Email: apostledr@alanpateman.com
Web: www.AlanPatemanMinistries.com

*Please include your prayer requests
and comments when you write.*

❖

Other Books

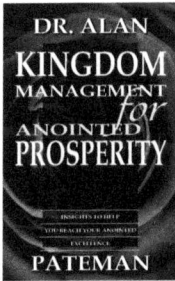

Kingdom Management for Anointed Prosperity

Dr. Alan Pateman reveals how we can avoid living in continual crisis due to mismanagement. Life happens to all of us, but how we handle it matters most. "Well done, good and faithful servant! You have been faithful with a few things; I will put you in charge [as manager] of many things. Come and share your master's happiness!" (Matthew 25:21).

ISBN: 978-1-909132-34-4, Pages: 144, Format: Paperback, Published: 2015
Also available in eBook format!

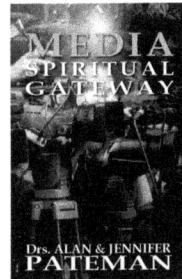

Media, Spiritual Gateway

Let's face it; we live in the era of fake news! It's always existed, but never been quite so prominent. Today it's an all-out-war between fact and political fiction. The media has been sabotaged by political activism. Gone are the days of impartiality and objective unbiased reporting, with many sources saying that true journalism is dead.

ISBN: 978-1-909132-54-2, Pages: 192, Format: Paperback, Published: 2018
Also available in eBook format!

Truth for the Journey Books

Millennial Myopia, From a Biblical Perspective

The standard for every generation is Jesus. However Millennial Myopia describes the trap of focusing everything on one particular generation or demographic cohort, at the exclusion and expense of all others. The Church cannot afford to make this mistake too. Loaded with research, this book takes readers on a journey of discovery, revealing the true nature of kingdom diversity.

ISBN: 978-1-909132-67-2, Pages: 216, Format: Paperback, Published: 2017
Also available in eBook format!

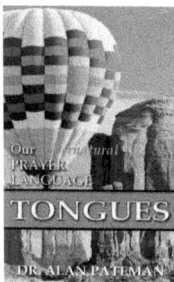

His Life is in the Blood

Blood is the trophy of every battle. The spilt blood of Jesus Christ is our trophy. It is our freedom from sin and bondage. Nothing can enter the blood-bought temples of the Holy Ghost!

ISBN: 978-1-909132-06-1, Pages: 152
Format: Paperback, First Published: 2007
Also available in eBook format!

TONGUES, Our Supernatural Prayer Language

In writing to the church at Corinth, Paul encouraged them to continue the practice of speaking with other tongues in their worship of God and in their prayer lives as a means of spiritual edification. "He that speaketh in an unknown tongue edifies, charges, builds himself up like a battery."

ISBN: 978-1-909132-44-3, Pages: 144, Format: Paperback, Published: 2016
Also available in eBook format!

LIFESTYLE UNIVERSITY

Raising Up
Christian Leaders

Dear Friends,

Have you considered becoming one of our international students? We are privileged to welcome you, from around the world, to "LifeStyle International Christian University" *(the teaching arm of Alan Pateman Ministries International)*. **An English speaking university** dedicated to your success; to see you trained and equipped to fully succeed in your God given Destiny.

It is our passion to raise up the leaders of tomorrow, who will have influence in all realms of authority, including the Body of Christ. Men and women of strategy, wisdom and true godliness, who'll stand with stature and maturity in this hour.

It's undeniable that in today's world, recognised education has become indispensable, therefore it is our desire to offer well balanced and well structured courses. Those that have been written by gifted and talented ministers of God, who seek to be inspired by God's Holy Spirit.

Consequently we have put together a **flexible curriculum,** designed both for correspondence students and campuses, which is a strategy to reach the distant learner; whether provincial, national or international. In fact we have many correspondence students from around the world, including a growing number of successful campuses, in various countries.

This is a growing platform, where men and women of dignity and passion, can grow and be established in their God given endeavours. As God is the healer of the nations, we pray and believe that many of our alumni will go on to **become world changers** in their own right.

We are proud of each and every one of our LICU students.
It would be our pleasure if you would join them on this incredible journey!

Doctor Alan Pateman

Alan Pateman Prof. Ph.D., D.Min., D.D., M.A., B.Th.
PRESIDENT AND CEO
www.licuuniversity.com www.cfeapostolicnetwork.com
Email: info@licuuniversity.com Mob: +39 366 329 1315

For more information visit our website/facebook or contact our office, using the details below:

Website: www.licuuniversity.com
Facebook: www.facebook.com/LICUMainCampus
Email: info@licuuniversity.com
Telephone: +39 366 329 1315

Alan Pateman Ministries
Presents

Conference

CONNECTING FOR EXCELLENCE Lucca Italy

An international apostolic
and prophetic network

YOUR HOSTS: ALAN PATEMAN   JENNIFER PATEMAN

apostledr@alanpateman.com, Tel. 0039 366 329 1315

WWW.ALANPATEMANMINISTRIES.COM

All Books Available

at

APMI PUBLICATIONS

Email: publications@alanpateman.com
*Also Available from Amazon.com
and other retail outlets.*

*If you purchased this book through Amazon.com
or other and enjoyed reading it, or perhaps one of
my other books, I would be grateful if you could
take a couple of minutes to write a Customer
Review, many thanks.*